The Veg Box

STEPHEN & DAVID FLYNN

THE HAPPY PEAR

The Veg Box

10 VEGETABLES, 10 WAYS

Photography by Maja Smend

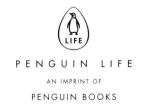

PENGUIN LIFE

AN IMPRINT OF

PENGUIN BOOKS

CONTENTS

INTRODUCTION

Vegetables are extraordinary miracles. You sprinkle a few seeds and allow Mother Nature to do her thing with sunlight and water, roll on a few weeks, and you have food: delicious fresh produce – cucumbers, tomatoes, pumpkins, kale, to name just a few. This book is a celebration of that miracle.

Growing up, we used to think of veg as boring and bland. When we changed to a plant-based diet twenty years ago it was like going through the keyhole into a whole new world, a world exploding with colour, abundant in flavour, succulent and sweet, tender and decadent. Veg have a language of sorts that we have decoded since our love affair began: how best to accentuate a certain veg's unique properties, how best to enhance its flavours, whether to steam, to bake, to grill, and what to season it with.

To say we are veg enthusiasts is an understatement. Veg has been our life for the last two decades, central to all that we have done. This book is a love letter to veg, our tribute to all the wonderful veg that have nourished us and satiated us over our lives. Whether you are newly interested in eating more veg or if you have had a lifelong affair with veg, this book has plenty in it for you.

Each of us has our favourite veg which we tend to gravitate towards – many of us have emotional relationships with potatoes, and maybe you feel comforted by mushrooms or happiest cooking carrots. We all have our go-to veg, ones that we know a few ways to make shine, and us in turn. In this book, we have chosen 10 of our favourite veg that are also most common in the UK and Ireland, and we have put together 10 delicious recipes for each one, all using no more than 10 ingredients.

Having a veg shop has forced us to really push these 10 veg to their limits, as there are often surplus supplies or gluts of produce. We have explored most of the conceivable and delicious iterations of what you can do with these 10 veg in these chapters, doing our best to include a breakfast, lunch, dinner and sometimes, where possible, even a sweet option! But instead of organizing the chapters by mealtime, as most cookbooks usually do, we have organized them instead by veg, with a full chapter of recipes for each one.

So if you find yourself with too many leeks or are wondering what to do with a beetroot from your veg box, this book is for you. Or if you have three carrots at the bottom of the fridge and need some inspiration for what to do with them, well, we have 10 great recipes using only 10 ingredients for you to try, from carrot and maple granola, to carrot and sesame burgers, to easy carrot cake cupcakes – we have you covered!

We all know that in order to eat well we should eat more veg and less processed, calorific food, but it's not always that easy. We know just how hard it can be to find inspiration to cook when you're faced with those three carrots at the bottom of the fridge. So we want this book to make eating healthy, mood-boosting veg easier, tastier and more inspiring than ever before. We have designed each chapter to show you new ways to cook these 10 incredible veg and to share ideas for how you can eat better food, both for your body and the planet. We hope they bring joy to your kitchen and change your relationship with veg for ever.

Eat seasonal

We love fresh veg. For the first five years after we set up The Happy Pear, we got up at 4.30 every morning to drive into the Dublin fruit market in Smithfield in our little red van to pick our produce for the day's trading ahead. We remember hunting around the market for the freshest cauliflowers, and our excitement when the first of the Irish strawberries would come in. It was a world of its own, a secret society of early-morning veg enthusiasts.

Dublin fruit market was a bustling, vibrant place back then, overflowing with action and life, with farmers delivering freshly picked produce to wholesalers, chefs and shopkeepers like ourselves, who were in search of the freshest veg and the best bargains. It was here that our love of veg was nurtured into the passion that we hold now. Seeing the fresh produce arriving from the surrounding countryside each morning made us feel so connected to the world around us and put us at the heart of something special.

Unfortunately, the market has pretty much closed down over a number of years, as our food system has fewer small independent shops and has become centralized around supermarkets and monopolies controlling the flow of our food. The problem with buying fruit and veg in supermarkets is that we have lost touch with that sense of what is fresh, seasonal, and what is local. We take it for granted that we can buy raspberries, tomatoes, swedes and pumpkins all year round, but they are being shipped from all over the world to supply that demand. The excitement for the taste of the first summer strawberries, or that autumnal hearty stew with the flavours from fresh root veg, has been lost as a result of convenience.

Whether you decide to sign up for a veg box and have a random selection of local, seasonal fresh veg delivered to your door, or simply select your shopping in the supermarket more consciously, we hope that the variety of veg in this book and the advice on when it's in season will help you connect again to the growers of this food and where it comes from, and bring an added appreciation to how you shop and eat it, all year round.

Eat for the planet

As fathers, we are worried. We worry that unless we start to address our current environmental crisis, to become more sustainable in our food choices, it is just a matter of time until the climate and soil change to such a degree that our children and future generations may not be able to grow food on this planet. According to landmark research from Oxford University, eating a plant-based or plant-centred diet is the single biggest thing you can do for the planet in terms of helping to reverse climate change. Better still, the more we shop locally for that veg and support smaller producers who grow diverse veg and care properly for their soil, the more sustainable the food system becomes.

Climate change can often feel like that overwhelming job that has been on your list for weeks – you know when there is that one thing that you just don't want to face and can't even imagine how you are going to start it, and you would much rather turn your back and hope it sorts itself? We think climate change and the current state of the environment are like that – it's a bit like the gorilla in the middle of the room that you have just got used to living with and working around. However, we are at a tipping point right now, and it is time to face the music and start to dance. The gorilla you have been ignoring is not happy and is crying for your attention.

But it doesn't need to feel so intimidating – how you eat is the single most important thing you can do to slow climate change. You don't have to throw everything away and transform overnight; eating more veg and less meat or fewer processed foods is a simple choice you can make every day – you just need to know how to cook it in a tasty and easy way that works for you.

Eating a plant-based diet also happens to be one of the best things you can do for your own personal health. Not only have we seen this in our own lives over the last twenty years, but we have also witnessed first-hand more than 50,000 people go through our online courses and discover the sheer positive power that a plant-based diet can have on your health, energy and wellbeing. Plus, knowing that you are helping to save the planet for future generations makes this doubly appealing.

Now it is time to start taking steps in this direction – you are holding a book that can help you take action as an individual to cook delicious plant-based food, to waste less, improve your health and in the process help save the planet. We hope that not only will these recipes show you new ways to cook your old favourites, but they will also introduce you to veg you haven't tried before. Whether you eat completely plant-based already or just want to find new, easy ways to get your 5-a-day, we want to help you enjoy eating more plants.

One of our favourite mantras is 'progress over perfection', and we think this is so true in terms of making changes to our food and lifestyle to make them more sustainable and kinder to the planet. We often feel overwhelmed when we look around our own veg shop and see that we're selling products in plastic, and that in winter most of the fruit is not in season and not grown locally, but it is about moving the dial in the right direction towards eating more plants and doing your best.

The other day my daughter was asking me about saving money and I was trying to explain to her that saving a little bit consistently over time is the best way to build up a good pot, and I think this is so true in the context of the planet. If we can consistently change our habits to make them more sustainable, we will save the most important thing of all, the planet that sustains life.

We want to be part of the solution and we are doing our best to walk our talk. Often we feel overwhelmed by how hypocritical we can be in terms of trying to embody the ideal, like using a lot of lentils and beans from other countries, eating avocados here in Ireland, heating the growing chambers in our indoor farm; however, when we do stop and reflect, here are some of the things we have managed to achieve.

We started an organic sourdough bakery, which had been a dream of ours for many years; we have made a real effort to source organic flour grown locally, where the farmer uses regenerative practices like no tilling and focuses on nurturing the soil. We went to visit Emma from Oak Forest Mills, where they grow heirloom varieties of grain and stone-mill them and we use these in our bakery.

We are in the process of expanding our farm to grow more organic veg, working in harmony with the land to build healthy biodiverse soil, and we will offer a community veg box scheme to link people from our community with the farm and their food. We see it as a vehicle to connect us and our community to the land and the seasons. We have talked to local education boards about including schools and special-needs kids as part of the weekly curriculum for the farm visitors, to really make it relevant as an example of connecting us more to our food.

We also use about a quarter tonne of fresh basil a week to make our famous pestos. Basil likes to grow in a warm dry atmosphere, so in summer we can buy this from local farmers in Ireland, but in winter we need to import it from much hotter countries, which makes it harder to source consistently and has a much higher environmental cost to it. We are in the process of starting an indoor vertical basil farm so that we can have a year-round consistent supply of basil with much less environmental impact. Our vans now run on natural compressed gas rather than petrol or diesel, with a lower environmental impact, and we are in the process of sourcing bio-diesel.

This is just the beginning of what we hope to achieve, and by no means have we done everything perfectly along the way, but we all have to start somewhere and be honest with ourselves about the decisions we are making. No one can solve any of the problems alone, so we hope that this book will show you the little changes you can start making, and the food you can start enjoying that will make a big difference. Together we can do this.

Waste less

We do our best to minimize the food we waste at home, in our shop and in our cafés, which is challenging but brings an opportunity to get creative. The very idea of this book came from our intention to find ways to reduce food waste. We've heard so many customers in our veg shop over the years asking what to do with kale or courgettes that a neighbour gave them, and this book is all about showing you new ways to make delicious meals out of common veg so that nothing has to go to waste.

Not only is it great for your wallet to get the most out of the food you buy, but reducing the amount of food you waste has a massive benefit for the health of the planet. Globally, food waste accounts for approximately 30% of all food produced, which is staggering when you think of how many people go hungry in this world. And it is not just the food that is wasted, it is the growers' time, the water and energy that have gone into growing the food, the energy used to transport it, the energy to store it, package it and sell it, and all these things contribute to global warming. Also, when food waste is sent to landfill the valuable nutrients that could benefit the soil via composting are not only lost, but can also cause further environmental harm. Organic compounds decompose anaerobically (without oxygen), releasing methane, a greenhouse gas that is approximately twenty-three times more potent than carbon dioxide.

Over the years we have found that the more we engage with our food, the story and the people behind it, where it came from, how it was grown and by whom, the less likely we are to waste it. For example, a friend of ours, Dan, grows most of the cherry tomatoes that we eat during summer. We know the amount of effort he puts into them, the time, commitment and resources, and knowing this makes us savour them and definitely not waste any of them.

This book is the most practical, reader-friendly book we have written, and as we were writing each chapter, focusing on the beauty of each individual ingredient, we wondered why we had never thought of this before! We are so excited for you to be holding this book and bringing it on your plant-based journey, whatever that looks like for you.

We really encourage you to cook these recipes, to share them with friends and family, to use the power of plant-based food to heal yourself and the planet, and to share and celebrate the variety and beauty of veg. Food has the ultimate power of bringing us together, connecting us to one another, to help nature recover and to completely transform our own health. What we eat can literally help save the planet, save you money and have you beaming with health. We hope you use this book as your guide, that you cook the delicious recipes and spread the important message of eating more veg, for you, for the planet and for future generations.

YOUR FOOD CHOICES AND THE ENVIRONMENT

You might have thought that the best thing you could do for the environment was to cut out plastic, stop flying or buy an electric car, but eating a plant-based diet, sourced as locally as possible, in fact has the biggest impact.

When we started The Happy Pear as a small veg shop, we didn't really think that we would become part of the global food system. We were all about local and seasonal food, but very quickly we started to realize that if we wanted to have a decent range to compete with the likes of the big supermarkets it would need to come from all over the planet. If we wanted to sell bananas or mangoes, for example, we had to accept that there is a huge transport industry behind getting these products to us that is emitting greenhouse gases and contributing to the climate crisis.

We quickly realized that most of the fruit in Ireland and the UK is imported, and quite a large portion of the veg too. Most of it travels in lorries on boats taking a number of days, meaning that most of this produce is a week or so old by the time you get it and has a lot of 'food miles' (the distance food travels from the time of harvesting until it reaches you) and resources used to get it to you. A few types of fruit and veg are air-freighted (yes, they literally get flown from the other side of the world to us), such as Peruvian asparagus for about eight months of the year, raspberries in our winter, green beans and sugar snap peas from Kenya. These are best to avoid when you're shopping because the food miles are astronomical and the environmental impact is huge.

What's in the box?

We remember buying a fancy box of exotic pineapples in the market one morning and bringing it back to find there was a pair of very exotic and colourful-looking frogs in the box that started to jump around our veg shop. This made us visually aware that these pineapples were from a very different climate than ours – they certainly weren't local frogs! This shift towards eating foods from further afield has happened just in our short lifetime; the first time we tasted an avocado, mango and even a pomegranate we were in our early twenties. These weren't foods that were part of our diet growing up, yet they are widely available today. This has led to older and younger people eating quite differently; for example, we have noticed in

recent years that only the older customers will demand 'local' veg like a swede, turnip or York cabbage, and they will know the different types of potatoes, while we tend to sell more sweet potatoes, avocados and Mediterranean veg, like peppers, than some of the local root veg. Avocados have a carbon footprint approximately five times bigger than bananas. However, to give another reference point here, lamb has a carbon footprint forty-six times higher than avocados.

Food miles can sometimes be misleading, as they don't factor in the environmental impact of animal foods versus fruit and veg. Local beef might seem a better environmental choice than avocados from Mexico, yet when you factor in the full environmental cost of emissions from farming to packaging and transportation, the local beef has a higher environmental impact in spite of the miles that the avocados have travelled. Whether you buy beef from local farmers or from the other side of the world, it typically has a much higher carbon footprint and environmental impact than fruit and veg and plant-based foods, even if the produce is from other countries – in fact, every kilo of beef creates 52kg of CO_2 (excluding methane, which would make it 100), compared to 2.5kg for every kilo of avocados. So the first question to answer when considering the environmental impact of your food is whether it is animal or plant-based, before considering the food miles.

When the time is right

In Italy we have always admired how they generally still eat seasonally – even in most supermarkets you only get what's in season and grown in Italy. I remember going hunting just outside Rome for wild asparagus when it came into season, with the kids and our Italian friends, Pietro and Katie, and was delighted to see it also available in local shops and even some of the supermarkets. They celebrate when the first of the wild asparagus is up, they start using fennel as soon as that season starts, and when blood-orange season in Sicily commences, you really know about it.

We all need food to survive. It is so central to our lives that most of us have an emotional relationship with it. We eat certain foods to celebrate, other foods when we feel good, or bad, when the sun shines or when it is wet and cold. We all have our comfort foods and easy meals that we can make without thinking, and so, when we are short on time and life takes over, many of our food habits and shopping trips tend to be very habitual and subconscious, with most of us eating the same type of foods each week. Studies say most of us have about six recipes that we rotate, and we can understand why – it makes life easier, especially if you have a family. But what if we slowly, one at a time, started thinking more consciously about these recipes and making them more plant-based, using more local ingredients without compromising on flavour? We would certainly see a massive improvement in our individual health, and it would mean a huge shift in favour of our environment.

While fruit and veg are much better choices than animal foods for the environment, there are still huge disparities in terms of the environmental impact and the sustainability of our choices. Next time you are in the supermarket, have a look at the label and see what is local and where the produce you buy is grown. Generally, the further away from you it was grown, the older the produce will be or the longer the amount of time it has been travelling.

Each fruit and veg has a season, a time and specific set of conditions that are optimal for it to grow in your local area. Fresh fruit and veg start to germinate and grow in spring and typically they are ready to eat at some stage in summer or autumn, though in the case of some veg like broccoli or Brussels sprouts, they like a bit of frost and the sharp cold of winter before they are ready to be picked. Depending on how close you get to the equator, this will dictate what will grow – the warmer the climate, the greater the diversity and the longer the growing season. Most veg and leafy greens grow better in more maritime climates like Ireland and the UK, whereas sweeter fruits like mango and pineapple like the sun. Try to be mindful of what is in season for you and lap it up when you can buy it as locally as possible. Some fruit and veg can never be grown locally to you, so use these sparingly and be aware of the food miles they've taken to get to your plate. We have information on the seasons for all 10 veg in the book, so that you can look out for the best time and places to get your hands on them and enjoy them at their freshest.

One summer, about fifteen years ago, we decided we were going to eat only local food for a month, as an experiment to try to 'walk our talk' a little more. We wanted to limit the food miles in our food. It was June, so the full bounty of the Irish summer hadn't started: there were no tomatoes or cucumbers or courgettes yet. We were limited to strawberries, greens such as cabbage and lettuce, potatoes, some onions, leeks and not that much else! We were young in our experience as chefs, so after our tenth night of 'sp-onion' – a dish of potatoes and onions – we packed it in and decided that we just needed more variety!

This is to say that, living in Ireland, we are limited by what grows here and can't get all the ingredients we are so used to eating. There are lots of greens like salad leaves, kale, cabbage, broccoli, root veg, and some fruit such as apples, pears, plums and berries, but when we started our veg shop we really wanted to try to expand this out. We constantly wondered whether there was a way to actually grow local bananas or fruits that are more exotic. We managed to grow an avocado tree that was the size of us, which we christened Jake; however,

he didn't like the wintertime in our cold cottage so he didn't last long. We partnered with a local farm, which had polytunnels full of local cherries, genuinely the best cherries we have ever eaten and grown in Ireland, and even peaches, yes, Irish peaches! Unfortunately, this particular variety of peach was hairy like a tennis ball and crunchy like an apple, not what we had hoped for, but it did encourage us that these more exotic stone fruits can be grown locally without non-renewably generated heat. There is hope, it just takes time and commitment.

The lack of diversity

We were alarmed to read, while researching this book, that there are somewhere in the region of 20,000 edible plants on the planet, yet just five plants make up about 75% of our globalized produce system. You can probably guess the five: sugar, corn, wheat (white flour), rice and soy. With the climate changing, and the rise in temperatures, droughts, storms and heatwaves, this lack of biodiversity in our global food system is a shocking statistic, and actually puts agriculture and our long-term nutrition at risk. It's even more upsetting when you think back to the potato famine in Ireland in the nineteenth century, when our ancestors depended on one variety of potato to feed the nation and the crops failed, leaving the country starving.

Biodiversity and growing a variety of fruit and veg are really important factors in terms not only of our physical health, but also the health of our food, the soil it comes from and food security. This last point means that people across the world can access the food they need to live happily and healthily, and is a growing global concern, as these top five plants are relied on more and more. Studies show that small farms that grow a diversity of crops tend to be much more productive in terms of the quantity and variety of food they can produce, as well as this diversity being very beneficial to the soil, animal and insect biodiversity, than monocropping farms that simply grow one crop. So by doing your best to choose more local and organic produce from small-scale farms that are growing a variety, you can literally help encourage more diversity of plants, animals and soil.

This is a lot to take in and consider when you are thinking about how to eat more veg, but overleaf we have shared a sustainable hierarchy that we do our best to follow, which lists all the different food choices we can make, and their impact on the environment.

OUR SUSTAINABLE HIERARCHY

1. Eat a plant-based diet or a plant-centred diet.

2. Eat a variety and diversity of plant-based foods for your health and to encourage biodiversity.

3. Prioritize eating local, organic and in-season produce. Do your best – there is no perfect solution and we know it can often be more limiting, but if you time it right the local foods in season are actually the cheapest and most delicious.

4. Choose local produce over imported organic options – this will have the least impact on the environment and keeps your money locally.

5. Choose imported organic produce over imported non-organic options to support more sustainable farming methods across the world.

6. Choose fruit and veg from anywhere over animal foods, as they will have a lower environmental impact, even comparing imported fruit and veg to local animal products.*

*An exception is when tomatoes are grown locally but outside of their season in heated glasshouses: these have a higher carbon footprint compared to those grown in season outside in the Spanish sun and then transported to the UK or Ireland.

GROWING VEG

When we first started our veg shop in 2004 we barely sold any organic fruit and veg. We were afraid they were too expensive and that customers would not want to pay for them. There were no organic suppliers in Dublin fruit market, and it was like an undercover operation to find organic fruit and veg suppliers. It was like swimming against the current. Slowly, as we started to become more confident that it was the better option in terms of our own health and the health of the planet, we realized there were others like us, so we started to find local organic suppliers. Roll on sixteen years and all we sell is organic produce, and our veg shop and cafés are all supplied by an organic farm.

Over the years, we used to go to big international food fairs to meet new suppliers and get inspiration – it was a lovely 'busman's holiday' that we looked forward to and got lots out of, meeting like-minded fruit and veg enthusiasts and food lovers. One of the most interesting distinctions we started to note was the difference between attending the world organic food fair versus the equivalent in non-organic. The world organic food fair, Biofach, was held in Nuremberg in Germany and, when we used to attend, it was very friendly and sustainability-focused, with lots of small producers all casually dressed. It was a really pleasant affair that we loved and got such a buzz from attending.

We also attended Fruit Logistica in Berlin, one of the world's leading fresh produce fairs – this one was all non-organic and the difference was stark. The majority of people there wore suits and traded 'commodities', buying big shipping containers full of melons or pineapples, and it was so much more about money. It was super-evident which side of the fence we were drawn to – while one was more about how much money you could make from fresh produce, the other seemed to be a nicer balance of passion for food and the planet, as well as it being a lucrative business.

Soil is magic

It is easy for us all to see soil as dirty, something that we try to scrape off our shoes before entering our home in winter. However, we ask you what is one of the most sophisticated pieces of technology on this planet? Forget our supercomputers or our electric cars or even our spaceships – these are all wonderful inventions, but one of the most sophisticated things on the planet is, in fact, our soil. It is one of the richest, most biologically diverse living things on the earth – in fact, there are more valuable bacteria in one teaspoon of soil than there are humans on earth. When you consider that 95% of our food is grown in topsoil, the top 20cm of soil, it is one of the most important components of our food system, and yet we cannot come close to replicating or synthesizing soil, as it takes roughly 500 years to make. Over the last fifty years, we have lost more than 50% of our topsoil due to many factors, including chemical farming, monocropping, tilling, lack of cover crops, to name a few. And even more shockingly, according to United Nations research, we have only sixty harvests left until all our topsoil is gone. When our topsoil dies and is infertile, it won't be long before we follow. Facts like this should remind us that we are part of nature and not separate.

Though we are now passionate about supporting the soil through responsible farming, when we were growing up, farming seemed like a backward, traditional industry. We remember getting a job picking potatoes on a farm in Kilcoole and hating it! It always seemed less sophisticated work compared to tech or getting a job in a city, where you work at a computer. But as we've got older we've realized it is one of the most important industries, because if we don't respect and farm with sustainable practices, we will lose the ability to grow the crops we need to feed and nourish ourselves. No amount of free Wi-Fi or Netflix is important if we don't have good-quality food.

Unfortunately, as technology has advanced over the last fifty years, it has become easier for companies to produce food for a lower price in a shorter time frame. These farming methods and use of chemicals are becoming more common and, while great for business, they are having a dramatic effect on the ecosystem. When we first started going to the Dublin fruit market as two highly enthusiastic twenty-four-year-olds we were amazed at the scale of everything, forklifts flying around like race cars and big forty-foot trucks delivering fresh produce. Reflecting back on it now, a big truck would come in with a container of nicely waxed oranges, stacked high with eighty boxes on a pallet, in same-sized boxes. 'Do you want 48s, 60s or 100s?' we'd be asked. Meaning do you want 48, 60 or 100 oranges per box, as they were all in different uniform sizes with different quantities in each box. It was like much of the fruit was coming from factories rather than farms. There was little soil or evidence that the produce came from the earth. They were even in shiny cardboard boxes. It was the same with peppers, tomatoes, and much of the other produce.

Similarly, in recent years, we visited a tomato 'farm', which was actually more like a tech lab. All the plants were grown in coconut coir or coconut husk rather than soil, with a feeding system that was linked back to a computer, which monitored and regulated the exact amount of food and light the plant got, in order to maximize the size and the colour of the fruit. Initially we were super-excited and couldn't wait to eat our weight in fresh produce, but we left feeling sad and worried about how mechanized and disconnected from nature our food system had become.

Please don't get us wrong, these technologies are amazing and the efficiencies are phenomenal; however, much of this approach to farming is disconnected from the earth and has forgotten about building biodiversity in soil and working with nature, rather than trying to control and dominate it. Most chemical fertilizers are based on N, P, K, nitrogen, potassium and phosphorus, and include many other nutrients, but they cannot mimic nature – with every teaspoon of soil packed with billions of different bacteria needed for our ecosystem to thrive, it is virtually impossible to recreate or sequence.

How we treat the earth

Today, in Europe and North America, roughly 70% of us live in cities and urban environments, largely detached from nature and our food. This detachment has made it easier to turn a blind eye to our broken food system, which has become hyper-mechanized and focused on maximizing profit and output at the expense of the soil and nature. Today's food systems, with chemical agriculture and monocropping (massive farms of one type of crop such as corn or wheat), are polluting our environment using chemicals, fertilizers and pesticides, eroding topsoil at a massive rate and significantly contributing towards turning soil into deserts.

One of the biggest agricultural causes of global warming is our current chemical farming system. It's a cyclical process in which farmers use chemical fertilizers to artificially feed the crops, then till the soil, releasing trapped carbon, which contributes to global warming, along with moisture loss. The lack of cover cropping – to protect the soil – in between harvests further dries out the soil. Over time, this approach leads to topsoil drying out and eventually being blown away in the wind. This was evident in the 1930s dust bowl, where a huge portion of the topsoil was blown away in the Midwest of the USA from excess monocropping and lack of cover cropping. Farmers are often forced into farming in this manner as they don't believe there is an alternative – they are often burdened by debt and sold the dream that to feed the world we need chemicals; however, the cost of this 'modern' approach to farming is the degradation of the land. We explain this process in more detail later.

The quality of our soil is also linked to our economies, which may sound a little far-fetched but, if you think of it, at the very root of our early economies, agriculture and soil quality were directly correlated to economic prosperity – if you had good land with rich, healthy soil, you could grow more food and sell more food. For millennia we have built settlements on lands that had rich and fertile soil, as life was easier to sustain there, and we could grow nutritious food easily. Today you may think this could not be the case, but there are many examples that illustrate this. According to research in the journal *Proceedings of the National Academy of Sciences* in 2021, more than a third of farmland in the Midwest of the USA has completely

lost its topsoil due to erosion. The loss of this topsoil has resulted in yields of corn and soybeans decreasing by 6%, meaning a loss of nearly $3 billion a year for farmers. This means less money to spend in the local economies – as the amount of topsoil declines, so does the surrounding economy.

As soil starts to erode and it loses its top layer, the microclimate starts to change. If you take a square metre of soil and make it bare of grass or plants, it will be much colder at dawn and much hotter at midday compared with a similar piece of soil covered with vegetation. By doing this you have changed the microclimate. When we do this to a large portion of the earth's land, by cutting down trees and ecosystems, we are changing the macroclimate of the whole planet. As our soils erode from mistreatment and turn to dust each year, food sources and economies are dramatically affected, forcing millions of people into poverty. According to the Intergovernmental Science-Policy Platform on Biodiversity and Ecosystem Service (IPBES), land degradation like this affects approximately 3.2 billion people around the world, which is over a third of the planet's population. Poor land leads to poor food, which in turn leads to poorer health and poor economies: it is all linked, and, you guessed it, the start of regeneration occurs with nurturing good soil.

We know that this might come across as very bleak, but in your hands there is a solution. Every time you eat you have the opportunity to support a system that supports soil health, more diversity and fewer carbon emissions. Try to choose more plant-based foods, use the recipes in this book for inspiration, choose more organic, more local produce, get to know your local farmers and look out for those using more regenerative farming practices; even try to grow some produce or join an allotment, and, most importantly, do your best. There is no perfect solution, but a lot can be achieved with many small steps.

Farming in the future

The industrial farming that we see now is a product of a time when there was an effort to shortcut or 'hack' nature. Post World War II, with the introduction of synthetic fertilizers, we could expect good yields from the land even if we had not been looking after the soil; these chemicals were the hack or shortcut that helped farmers skip developing diversity and health in their soil and they could still get good yields from the land. The problem is that over time, because the problem of soil diversity and soil health was not addressed, the farmer became more and more dependent on these chemical inputs of fertilizers and pesticides to produce the quantities demanded of them. This comes at the expense of the soil health, their own health and the health of their families, but it is impossible to leave this cycle. Our food system, like other aspects of our modern culture, can be overly focused on appearance and efficiency, and unfortunately has forgotten about the complexity of the soil and the important harmonious balance that is required if we are to pass on nourished land to our future generations.

We at The Happy Pear have been aware of this for some time. Our brother Darragh, who started working with us in the veg shop, was particularly disappointed by seeing how so much of the veg we sold was coming from abroad and how little was actually grown here in Ireland. We had also expected more, because Ireland has this image of people being close to the land and there being lots of green pastures, but the reality is that little of this is for growing vegetables or fruits. Darragh was always amazed at how Holland is one of the world's biggest exporters of vegetables and yet it is almost half the size of Ireland with almost four times the population! So when he finished studying, he joined us on The Happy Pear team with the goal of growing more produce here in Ireland and encouraging others to do so as well.

At the time, he was doing triathlons at a serious level and was eating a lot of sprouted seeds, sprouted beans, sprouted grains and wheatgrass juice to help with his recovery from all the training. He really started to see and feel the benefits, so we started our sprout farm in a couple of converted shipping containers and called it The Happy Pear Living Foods. At first Darragh simply supplied The Happy Pear, our shop and café in Greystones, and slowly over time other shops said they'd like to sell them and a small business was forming.

The farm has evolved over the years to supplying SuperValu, one of Ireland's biggest supermarkets, and getting organic certification for some of our products. But we always felt this wasn't the farm that Darragh first envisioned, so at the time of writing we are in the process of buying land to start our future farm. It will be six acres and the dream is to grow organically and regeneratively, focusing on nourishing the soil and growing the biodiversity of the land. We have many goals for the impact that the farm can have on the area, which we will touch on later.

Gut health, soil health and the health of our food

We have had more than 20,000 people through our online Healthy Gut Course and Gut Health Revolution Course, which we created with our friend, consultant gastroenterologist Dr Alan Desmond, and dietician Rosie Martin.

Recent developments in gut health research have shown just how crucial the gut is for our overall health and, after soil, our gut is the second most biologically diverse area of life known on this planet. It is believed that we have approximately 10 trillion human cells and are host to approximately 100 trillion bacteria and microorganisms, mainly existing in our gut, making us more of a host than anything else. We are inherently dependent on the health of all this bacteria that we are host to. We all like to believe that we are self-determining, independent individuals, but in reality our health and wellbeing are greatly linked to that of our gut microbiome (the collection of bacteria and microorganisms that live in our gut and throughout our bodies). The reality is that our microbiome plays a significant role in our wellbeing – 70% of our immune-system cells are based in our microbiome – and it also has a significant impact on the food you desire, your emotional state and your resilience to disease, to name just a few of its functions. What does this have to do with food and soil, we hear you say?

Well, the single biggest thing you can do for your microbiome health is to eat a diversity of plant-based foods, namely fruit, veg, beans, wholegrains, nuts and seeds. Your microbiome feeds on fibre as a prebiotic, which you only get from whole plant foods, so when we eat these foods we are directly feeding our gut the goodness it needs to thrive. Even better, if the fruits, veg, beans and wholegrains are grown in healthy soil that is diverse and rich in microorganisms, the benefits of these foods are compounded. It doesn't just benefit our own personal health, but with healthy soils that absorb and maintain rainwater and are cover-cropped, they will sequester more carbon and help to reduce further climate change and help rebuild a healthy natural world.

Biodiversity is a key concept in gut microbial health as well as in soil health. What is happening to much of the biodiversity of our soil, being destroyed by excessive pesticide usage and industrial farming, is also being reflected in what is happening to our own gut ecologies.

A rich and diverse gut microbiome is a key driver of human health and happiness. The limitless natural spaces in which humans evolved – forests, fields, beaches, and mountains – are the ultimate sources of that richness and diversity. According to Dr Alan Desmond, the changes that come with urbanization – lack of exposure to nature, the standard Western diet, increased antibiotic use, and environmental pollution – have all combined to take a serious toll on our gut microbial health. These twenty-first-century changes in our gut ecology have been linked to many chronic diseases, including inflammatory bowel disease, auto-immune conditions and asthma. Though it might seem like progress, our gut microbiomes have been suffering as we have gradually evolved to enjoy home comforts, live in clean houses and eat processed foods.

While antibiotics prescribed by a doctor are incredibly important and often life-saving, a single course of certain antibiotics can dramatically reduce your gut microbial richness and diversity. But they aren't just used in humans. Globally, approximately 60–70% of all antibiotics are used in animal farming because it was found that by giving animals antibiotics their weight could increase by as much as 15%, which means more potential for profit. So

even if you are not taking antibiotics, you may be getting them if you are eating animals or animal products.

Thankfully, Dr Alan has some good news on this front: your gut microbes are tougher than you think! In most cases your gut microbial balance begins to restore itself within weeks after taking antibiotics. So by focusing on a varied plant-based diet, spending time in nature, and maybe adding some fermented foods, you can help your gut microbes to flourish once more. No expensive probiotic supplements required.

Sadly, as farming has become more efficient and more industrial, the nutrition in our food has been diminishing. Soil degradation from industrial farming is affecting its nutritional value. Fruit and veg grown decades ago were actually richer in vitamins and minerals than the varieties most of us get today. A study from the University of Texas, looking at nutritional data from 1950 to 1999, compared the nutrients in forty-three different fruit and veg and found that six out of thirteen nutrients had decreased in nutritional value over that fifty-year period. They found that a key reason for this was because the focus of industrial farming practices was size, speed of growth, extended shelf life and pest resistance, but with a deficiency of focus on increasing nutrition.

A similar study in the UK looking at the period 1930–1980, published in the *British Food Journal*, found that in twenty veg the average calcium content declined by 19%, potassium by 14% and iron by 22%. Another study also concluded that you would have to eat twenty-one oranges to get the same amount of vitamin A our grandparents would have got from a single orange.

This decline in nutrition is not entirely due to soil degradation but also in part to the globalized food system. Varieties are chosen because they have a longer shelf life, are more aesthetically pleasing and grow quicker, as opposed to being grown because they are the most nutritious variety. There are some incredible producers out there cultivating fruit and veg for their flavour rather than their monetary value. We have long admired a chef in New York, Dan Barber, who grows older varieties of fruit and veg exclusively for flavour. Also, Jack Algiere grows carrots on his farm that have a Brix score (a scale to measure the sweetness of produce) of 16.9 – normal carrots might have a Brix score of 6–8, so his are more than twice as sweet as conventional carrot, as well as bursting with minerals. Dan Barber points out that Brix also indicates the presence of healthy oil and amino acids, proteins and minerals that are so critical in flavour. Jack Algiere sums it up nicely: 'The development of flavour and the health of the plant are the same thing, you don't get one without the other.'

What can you do about this?

Here is the empowering bit – every time you go to purchase food, or eat something, you can choose which system or which world you want to support: a system that nourishes and regenerates the soil or one that strips the topsoil away and releases more carbon into the atmosphere. By choosing food grown by organic farming (ideally using regenerative practices) you are choosing a better world.

We eat food many times a day, and each time is an opportunity to cultivate a conscious relationship with our land, farming, food, earth, climate, and our future and the generations that hopefully are yet to come. It's not just what you choose to eat, it is as much what you choose not to eat. Where you choose to buy from is also important – was it grown using regenerative practices, was the soil healthy or was it grown in soil devoid of life?

Climate change and our current environmental crisis are an opportunity for us to reflect and amend our ways; they are a calling to reconnect back to the earth, to the soil, to biodiversity. Mother Nature, the planet, the environment needs all our help, and we believe that if we connect back to the natural world, hopefully through this process we can all connect back to ourselves and one another.

FOOD WASTE

After eating a plant-centred or plant-based diet, the second biggest thing you can do for the environment is not to waste or throw out the food you buy. It sounds so basic and simple, and of course no one wants to throw away food, that would be just like throwing away money. Well, food waste costs the average household €500–700 a year and is made up of lots of little bits, such as those bananas that you didn't get around to eating and that went bad, the head of lettuce or bag of salad that you forgot about, the tomato that went soft and mouldy. We see the challenges in our own houses and in our cafés – it is often easier to simply throw it out, but there is immense satisfaction in saving the planet, saving money and being more sustainable with a little imagination around prepping our food.

We are always looking for uses for every part of our produce and how we can avoid wasting any of it. We started a juice bar in the back of our veg shop, where we would make fresh fruit and veg juices and smoothies. It was great in that we could use any 'ugly' fruit and veg, and it really helped minimize waste from the veg shop. We then ended up with loads of waste compost from all the juices and knew this was a useful resource for something. After a while we realized that a good use might be to feed it to our friend's huge pet pig, so we started to bring the compost up to him, which worked well for a good while until the pig wouldn't eat orange peels any more and the farm smelled like a citrus grove! Another friend of ours, Doug McMaster, who founded Silo (arguably the world's first zero-waste restaurant, which was in Brighton but is now in London), says 'waste is a lack of imagination' and we tend to agree. One person's waste is another's resource, and there are so many ways to create more closed-loop food systems.

We find the more we are connected to our food, to the farmer, to the land, the less likely we are to waste it. Steve's parents-in-law in Poland live on a farm and grow nearly all their food, and they have done this all through their lives. If you go down to their basement it is filled with a 'farmacy' full of pickled and fermented food – they are masters at preserving fresh fruit and veg and ensuring there is no waste. They live in harmony with the land and their food. Food waste is not a word in their language – if you grow and nurture it, you will eat it and certainly not waste it. We think food waste only exists as a result of us being disconnected from our food, where it comes from and the effort that is taken to grow it.

At The Happy Pear we have tried to nurture relationships with local farmers so that we understand where everything in our shop has come from, and the struggles they go through to grow the food, whether it's too much rain, too little rain or stormy winds blowing down their tunnels. This gives us a better appreciation for the food that was grown, where it comes from and what it took to grow it, and therefore we are determined not to waste it. We encourage you to connect to the food you buy, to understand where it was grown and who the farmer is. What type of farming do they practise? Do they use chemicals? Or do they work more harmoniously with the land, building the soil strength and nutrition?

According to environmental author Paul Hawken, if we eliminated food waste we would have more than enough food for not only the population now but also for the population expected in 2050. We produce more than enough food to feed everyone on this planet, yet every day one third of the world's food is wasted. That equates to 1.3 billion tonnes, which is 130,000,000,000kg, and you probably know what a kilo of bananas/potatoes looks like! If food waste were a country, it would be the third biggest contributor to climate change.

Fresh fruit and veg account for the greatest amount of your waste, at around 30% of your household food wastage. We wrote this book to help you overcome this problem and to give you ideas for what to do with that lonely bunch of kale in the bottom of the fridge or those beetroots or courgettes that a friend gave you. There is always a clever way to use them up, so we hope these pages inspire you to think a little outside the box and accept the challenge to make food waste a thing of the past.

How to reduce food waste

Most of us would prefer to have a little too much food rather than too little – it's normal, and is actually down to our evolution and fear of food scarcity. However, overestimating how much we will eat, or getting just a bit more in case, is what leads us to waste vast quantities of food. This is why getting it right in terms of the amount of food you buy, cook and eat is one that needs conscious consistent consideration to move the dial. But if you do, you will save yourself and the planet at the same time. On the next page we've shared our top tips on how to do just that.

9 SIMPLE WAYS THAT YOU CAN REDUCE YOUR FOOD WASTE

1. **Take a 'shelfie'** – Knowing what you already have at home in the fridge or the cupboard makes you less likely to buy too much.

2. **Don't shop when you are hungry** – This sounds really basic, but you will be more considerate and less susceptible to deals and offers and 'just in case' foods.

3. **Plan ahead of time** – Try to be purposeful when shopping for ingredients for a specific meal. Meal plans can result in much less food waste than simply buying to stock your shelves – make a plan for the week, and know what you are going to cook/eat/prepare.

4. **Follow 'use by' dates and not 'best before'** – 'Use by' is typically for fresh foods and is most important to follow; 'best before' dates give you an idea of how long foods will last before they lose quality. Most products will last beyond their 'best before' date if they are stored properly. 'Best before' is put on tinned beans and almonds, for example, foods that don't typically fall into the same category and are generally fine to eat – just use your common sense.

5. **If you have kids, factor in their tastes** – Let's face it, it is challenging feeding kids. In our houses the most waste comes from kids not eating what we had hoped they would eat. Sometimes this is understandable – upon reflection, of

course they weren't going to eat a spicy Thai curry. A lot of younger kids just like simple food, so by factoring this in and planning ahead of time you can save on food wastage.

6. **Learn to ferment/pickle your veg** – Fermenting and pickling have been used for centuries to preserve fresh veg in order to enjoy them during the winter. If you have ever had sauerkraut or kimchi or even apple cider vinegar, these are fermented foods. It's quite straightforward – all you need is a jar, some salt or some vinegar, and whatever you want to preserve!

7. **Use your freezer** – A freezer is a great ally in terms of minimizing food waste. We use our freezers all the time, especially for leftover dinners, which you can then defrost and eat another night.

8. **Don't over-serve at mealtimes** – Get in the habit of starting with a smaller portion and taking more if you want – this is particularly relevant if you have kids. Any extra can be kept for the next day or could be frozen.

9. **Compost your food waste** – Composting leftover food is a beneficial way to reuse food scraps, turning food waste into energy and soil for plants.

Dealing with food waste is an opportunity to become creative, to help your money to go further, to help do your bit for the planet. It is a habit and a skill really worth honing and refining, and by doing so you are likely to inspire others to do the same. Some of the most wasted foods are veg, which is partly why we wanted to write this book – to help you do your bit for nature and save money by improving your health at the same time!

Food waste and The Happy Pear

Food waste has many layers to it, and there are new innovations on how to solve this problem being created all the time. This year we plan to invest in a biodigester, a living 'machine', which is essentially a large suspended trough with a door on it that is the perfect temperature and environment to break down food waste and turn it into living compost. The beauty is, we can add any waste that our customers don't eat in the cafés, along with the compostable packaging, as well as all the food waste such as peels and stalks from our kitchens. Then in 24–48 hours this biodigester will turn what is sometimes food waste heading to landfill into compost to be used on our farm! Sounds cool, right? We are excited about this and are looking forward to kicking this project off. Of course, this is on an industrial scale that isn't suitable for everyone, but it's great to know that these are options for all hospitality venues to dramatically reduce their impact on the environment.

COMMUNITY AND CONNECTION

When we finished university, we first considered becoming investment bankers or accountants to pursue material success. But when it came to signing up to meet one of the big accountancy firms we hesitated, questioning if it was what we really wanted to do. Instead, we went abroad. While travelling and exploring, we found more of what gave us meaning. We discovered how food connected us to ourselves, provided nourishment and inspiration, connected us to the land and brought us together. It was as if something was awakening in us.

Growing up, we never considered where our food came from or how it was farmed – we simply ate for energy and for pleasure. As we dug in deeper, we realized that food touched a lot more than simply our own health and taste buds, that it could literally be the building blocks for a healthier, happier, more connected world – and it was on this basis that we started The Happy Pear. Food has an incredible power to bring people together, to connect us. We remember sharing food with Buddhist monks from Vietnam at our café, with special-needs kids, with homeless people and even with the president of Ireland, and the simple act of sitting together, of communicating, is a deeply connecting experience.

In recent years, we have seen a rise in anxiety, depression and loneliness in society. We did a schools tour around Ireland in 2019, talking to thousands of kids and trying to inspire them to eat more veg and live more sustainably. When we spoke with the principals of the schools, each one of them mentioned the rise in mental-health issues among their pupils. Even in our business, we have seen people call in sick saying that they couldn't work due to anxiety, which had previously never happened. It is estimated that 15% of the population suffer from loneliness, which can have a similarly negative impact on health to smoking fifteen cigarettes a day, and in the UK in 2018 there was even a minister for loneliness appointed at governmental level to address this epidemic. These are all unsettling facts that we want to find the solution to.

In our experience food can be a strong driving force to help us connect with one another, connect us to nature, and build community and become part of that solution. We ran a four-week study in a local school with 120 sixteen-year-olds, where we encouraged them to eat as much plant-based food as possible by talking to their parents and teachers about how and what to cook. We encouraged them to un-process their diet as far as possible, we tracked their sleep, their activity level and their phone usage, and we even cooked them soup on Fridays so that they could eat together. It was a huge success in terms of helping the students feel better in themselves and understand some of the habits that can help buffer against anxiety and stress.

Apple pie is the answer

I'm sure you remember the Greystones bumper apple crop of 2008? Odds are you don't, but that year we had lots of local people drop bags of apples from their gardens into our veg shop. They just couldn't face watching them rot and asked us to use them. We decided to share the love, and we gave them out for free. Granny Orr, a local lady and our fairy godmother, took some of the apples and baked us an apple pie and it was magic. The next day another lady, Mrs Murphy, baked us an apple pie and it wasn't quite as good as Granny Orr's, and when she found out, she was devastated! We realized how competitive people could be in terms of their apple-pie-making skills, so we thought let's have an apple-pie festival to celebrate apple season and have a baking competition!

We asked Steve's landlady, Betty Lowe, who was head of the local horticulture society, Tony, who was a professional baker, and the great Frank Doyle, a retired butcher, to be the judges. We didn't really use social media back then, so we did the next best thing and put an ad in the local parish bulletin, put some posters on lampposts around the town, and told anyone who came into the shop that we were having the inaugural apple-pie baking festival and to help themselves to free apples to make an entry. We ended up getting about thirty-five different apple pies as entries, from traditional ones, to crumbles, to Dutch-style pies, to strudels. Fittingly, the prize was an apple tree. Most importantly, the whole village came together to celebrate with one another. We've run our annual apple-pie competition for over twelve years now, in an effort to build community and celebrate apple season, which we love so much.

The apple-pie festival each year brings the whole community together to focus on what connects us – a love of food and delicious apple pies! It also reminds us how connected we are as humans to the natural world, its seasons and the food that is produced throughout the year, which is sometimes so easy to forget. In fact, when we were doing our school tour some of the kids believed that broccoli grew in supermarkets – which was a reminder of the importance of communities coming together around real, natural food.

Having a veg shop and café in a small town, we quickly realized how dependent we were on our local community and how important it was to cultivate this interdependence. We knew we needed to do a good job at serving our locals, stocking what they wanted, making delicious food, giving them ideas of what to do with certain veg, otherwise they wouldn't shop or eat with us. We realized that it is a symbiotic relationship.

We used to serve lunch in the café and never really sold breakfast – we reckoned that Greystones is a commuter town and most people have their 'brekkie' at home before their day starts. We used to make a big pot of porridge for the team and ourselves each morning and it was always such a treat on cold mornings when we were just back from the veg market. One day Sally, our manager at the time, said why don't we sell porridge? So we trialled giving away free porridge for a week to see what happened. Customers loved it – they found it strange for a business to be offering food for free, but it felt like a really nice thing to do for the community, to put a smile on people's faces and bond over food. That week was over fourteen years ago now, and hundreds of thousands of bowls of porridge later, it's still a firm favourite amongst the locals! This simple act has encouraged more trust, more connection with our community, and a more open dialogue about community and how food can really bring us together.

Harvest season

My wife, Justyna, (Steve here), comes from a small farming community in rural Poland. She remembers growing up harvesting wheat by hand, where they really worked with nature, focusing on soil health and crop rotation. They would grow virtually everything they ate and when something was from a shop it was labelled as 'kupione', which translates as bought from a shop, implying not of good quality! She often remembers how during harvest season the neighbours would all help each other get the precious harvest in before it got wet. When I've visited in recent years I always find it odd when Justyna's dad takes out the tractor and suits up to spray the fields with fertilizer and pesticides. It seems strange how even this small town in Poland, which once practised traditional farming methods, worked with nature and natural rhythms, and focused on soil health, now uses chemical fertilizers and pesticides like much commercial farming.

Back when we had a cherry farm, we used to bring our team down with their families at harvest time to pick cherries and revel in the sheer abundance of nature. It was a staff party of sorts, picking cherries with friends and family, laughing, spending time in nature – it was good for the soul and really connected our team with the farm we were growing them on.

Having a veg shop with a consistent stock of produce with a short shelf life forced us to become very social and to build a large community! When we order too much produce, we feel a responsibility to use it, so we will make up pots of soup and give it out to customers, drop it into neighbours, invite friends over to share in the glut rather than see it go to waste.

The dream for our farm that we talked about earlier is to create a centre that brings us all closer to our food source, a place for our communities to learn more about growing veg and working with the soil. It will also be a model to teach other farmers how to move from animal agriculture or industrial methods of farming to producing vegetables in a more harmonious relationship with nature, as hopefully public demand continues to shift to a more plant-based diet.

We want to set up Community Support Agriculture (CSA), where people can prepay at the start of the season for a weekly box of seasonal veg, which they will get during the growing season. This would support the farm to buy seeds and then each month they would be invited to come up and see the farm, pick some produce, meet the other members of the farm, to feel a part of it.

Our ultimate belief is that food can connect you to nature, to the land, to other people. It is one of the essentials of life and something that is so easy to do mindlessly, to not give a thought to how or where it came from. There are lots of smaller-scale community farms starting to pop up that encourage more biodiversity, healthy soils, tasty delicious produce, along with farm visits too. We believe that the more you can connect to where your food is grown, to who grows it, to the land, the more it will have a hugely positive impact on your life, your health, your mental health and the health of the planet.

A FINAL NOTE ON COOKING

We want you to share our passion for veg, so we have made these recipes as simple as possible in order for them to be easy and fun for anyone and everyone to cook at home. We've made sure that our recipes use no more than 10 ingredients, and have used just a few different spices and herbs throughout the book so that you don't end up with a long shopping list every time you want to try something new. These 10 key ingredients don't always include salt, pepper and oil, so remember to have those to hand. We suggest toppings and pairings for most dishes, but you should feel free to enjoy them in a way that suits you and what you have available. There are no rules, just great food!

We often cook with as little oil as possible because of how calorifically dense it can be and because it's a refined food. However, there are many recipes throughout the book that call for oil, as it raises the surface temperature of the pan and enables more caramelization and flavour development. In some places we have specified the oil you should use, but where we just say 'oil' you can use whatever you have to hand. Extra virgin rapeseed oil/canola oil is one of the best health-wise when living in Ireland and the UK, as it is grown locally and has a lower saturated fat than most oils. The healthiest option in terms of cooking is to use no oil and get your fats from wholefood sources such as nuts, seeds, avocados, olives, but by using oil you can develop more flavour and add more calories, which leads to more satiation. In essence there is a trade-off, and you have to decide which do you value more – health or flavour?

№. 1

AUBERGINE

Aubergines are one of our favourite veg, but they are often misunderstood.

Technically, an aubergine is a fruit, as it grows from a flowering plant and has a seed in it; but, just like courgettes and tomatoes, we use it as a vegetable. Aubergines are called eggplants in North America, but that name actually originated from the UK when the first aubergine arrived there, which was white and egg-shaped.

Often, when aubergines are undercooked, they can end up rubbery and lacking any flavour, hence they can get a bad reputation. With the recipes in this chapter we show their versatility, their incredible texture when cooked right, and their ability to carry flavour, especially savoury notes. We make aubergine 'bacon' for a BLT (page 52), there are delicious satay aubergine skewers (page 55), we use it for bakes like the parmigiana (page 63) and the layered aubergine and lentil bake (page 61), as well as lots more.

Aubergines are part of the nightshade family, along with tomatoes, peppers and potatoes. They come in a variety of colours, including green, white, purple-striped and even orange, and many sizes, from the shape we are probably most familiar with, to long and slender ones, to the Thai green-pea variety that is the size of a lime. We remember the first time we got graffiti aubergines in the shop – these are a smaller variety with a speckled white- and purple-coloured skin – they were so beautiful we didn't want to cook them! Of course, we did eventually and they were delicious!

Aubergines are celebrated in warmer climates from Italy to India. In Greece, they make moussaka, in France, they make ratatouille, and in Italy, you will be sure to come across melanzane parmigiana. In this chapter we take inspiration from how aubergines are cooked across the world, and put our own twist on some of these classic dishes for you to enjoy. We'll show you how to make sticky umami aubergine for the arrabbiata penne dish (page 53), how to char it for an epic lentil salad (page 57), and how to bake it with spiced harissa for plenty of flavour (page 67).

BUYING & STORING

When we first started our vegetable shop back in 2004, people didn't really buy aubergines – they were seen as exotic, and customers weren't familiar with cooking them. This meant that each week we would have lots of them turning, and so over time we found all sorts of new ways to cook with them.

When shopping for aubergines, try to choose ones that feel firm and have vibrant skins. Blemishes and odd shapes are fine, just avoid ones that are spongy. Another thing to look for is that the green tip should ideally have a strong colour on it – this is an indication of freshness. Aubergines store well at room temperature but keep longer in the fridge.

GROWING

The reason why aubergines are traditionally seen as exotic in the UK and Ireland is that they require lots of heat and summer sun to grow. This was why they were seldom planted or grown on these islands in the past, and in the rare times that they were, most people didn't know what to do with them!

With modern developments they can grow well in the UK and Ireland, but only under glass or in a tunnel. They are usually planted in early spring in glasshouses or tunnels and come to fruit in late summer, from July to early October after lots of warm summer sunshine. In warmer climates they can be grown outside glasshouses or tunnels but can take a little longer to grow.

COOKING

In the past, older varieties of aubergine needed salting, as they had a bitter taste. Today, there is no need for salting, as modern aubergines have had the bitterness bred out of them. They are absolutely beautiful grilled or roasted: try the grilled aubergine, roasted red pepper and lentil salad (page 57) for a wonderful introduction to grilled aubergines and how they can carry that charred soft delicate flavour. Aubergines are soft and somewhat porous in texture, and as a result are great at absorbing flavours. They are famous for soaking up loads of oil, so beware of this when cooking if you want to cook with less oil or fat. We love them marinated or cooked with tamari or soy sauce for that deep umami taste, like the easy aubergine, butter bean and spinach curry (page 64), where we fry them and cook them in tamari to give them that deeper flavour. Cutting aubergines makes them discolour quite quickly, so prepare them just before cooking. Try the chilli peanut aubergine noodle dish (page 58), where we cook mushrooms with aubergines to show their similarity of texture and how well they both absorb the wonderful, sweet, acid peanut sauce.

NUTRITION

Aubergines are high in fibre and water, and low in calories. Most people don't get their recommended daily intake of fibre; in fact, of the recommended 30g a day most people are only eating 18g. Fibre traditionally was just associated with being beneficial for digestion, but in the recent decades it has also been found to be a prebiotic, which is the food that the bacteria in our microbiome feed upon and that encourages more of the beneficial microbes to grow as opposed to the less beneficial ones.

Aubergine 'Bacon', Lettuce and Tomato Sandwich

This is our take on the classic BLT. When we were growing up, Mom used to pride herself on her BLT sandwiches and this makes the most wonderful nostalgic lunch for us. The idea of aubergine 'bacon' might sound silly, but it really holds that salty, umami, smoky flavour and tastes wonderful. Just use store-bought barbecue sauce and vegan mayo to save time.

6 INGREDIENTS

1. 1 medium aubergine
2. 2 ripe tomatoes
3. 4 tbsp barbecue sauce (page 276)
4. 4 slices of bread
5. 80ml vegan mayo (page 275)
6. 50g rocket or iceberg lettuce

Preheat the oven to 190°C fan/210°C/gas 5. Line two baking trays with baking parchment.

Slice the aubergine lengthways into ½cm-thick strips, then cut them in half again lengthways so they are the size of a strip of bacon. You will get around 16 slices.

Slice the tomatoes into ½cm-thick slices and sprinkle with a pinch of salt.

In a bowl, mix 2 tablespoons of olive oil with the barbecue sauce, add a pinch of salt, and mix well. Add the aubergine slices to the bowl and coat in the sauce.

Carefully add a single layer of coated aubergines to the lined baking trays. Bake for 10 minutes, then carefully turn the aubergines so they cook evenly. Bake for a further 5 minutes. Remove from the oven and set aside.

Lightly toast the bread and spread a generous dollop of vegan mayo over 1 side of each slice of toast (approx. 20ml per slice).

Add a layer of tomatoes to 2 of the slices of toast, followed by a layer of aubergine bacon and finally a nice even layer of lettuce. Put the other 2 slices of toast on top, then cut in half and enjoy!

Sticky, Spicy Aubergine Penne

These sticky, sweet umami aubergines really balance out the spicy tomato sauce and help elevate a traditionally simple dish. This is loosely based on an arrabbiata sauce, which originates from the Lazio region of Italy and the name of which refers to the 'angry' spice of the chilli-loaded tomato sauce. If you don't love spice, just reduce the amount of chilli.

10 INGREDIENTS

1. 2 medium aubergines

2. 3 tbsp maple syrup

3. 2 tbsp tamari or soy sauce

4. 2 cloves of garlic

5. 1 tsp chilli flakes or chilli powder, or ½ a fresh chilli

6. 200g wholemeal penne, or pasta of choice

7. 1 x 400g tin chopped tomatoes

8. 4 tbsp tomato purée

9. ¼ tsp red wine or balsamic vinegar

10. a handful of fresh basil, to serve

Preheat the oven to 200°C fan/220°C/gas 7. Line a baking tray with baking parchment.

Using a serrated knife, slice the aubergines into bite-size squares (approx. 1½ x 1½ x 1½cm. Put them into a bowl with 2 tablespoons of olive oil, the maple syrup and the tamari, and mix until well coated.

Spread the aubergines out evenly on the lined tray so that everything has space to bake. Bake for 25 minutes.

Peel and finely chop the garlic. Chop the fresh chilli, if using. Bring a medium-sized saucepan of water to the boil. Add a pinch of salt and cook the pasta on a high heat until slightly al dente, according to the packet instructions. Drain, keeping a little of the pasta water.

Heat 1 tablespoon of oil in a saucepan on a medium heat. Add the chilli and heat for about 1 minute, then add the chopped garlic and cook for 1 minute, until it starts to turn golden. Add the chopped tomatoes and tomato purée, mixing well. Bring to the boil, then reduce to a simmer for 5 minutes, stirring occasionally. Add the vinegar and a pinch of salt and ground black pepper.

Remove the baked aubergines from the oven. Add the cooked pasta to the tomato sauce, along with half the sticky aubergines, and mix until the sauce coats each piece of pasta. Add a little of the pasta water, 1 tablespoon at a time, until it reaches a nice texture that is not too thick and not too thin.

Divide between two bowls, top with the remaining aubergines and add a little drizzle of olive oil and a few basil leaves.

AUBERGINE

53

Sweet Satay Aubergine Skewers with Asian-style Slaw

These are great cooked on the barbecue or griddle pan, and are fab finger food for a gathering of any type. We love to serve these with the smashed roasted potatoes on page 254 and a simple salad. It's really important that the aubergines are fully cooked, to ensure you get that wonderful soft delicate texture.

10 INGREDIENTS

1. 9 tbsp peanut butter or almond butter
2. 150ml coconut milk
3. 4½ tbsp tamari or soy sauce
4. 1½ tbsp maple syrup
5. juice of 1 lime
6. 1½ tsp grated ginger
7. 2 medium carrots
8. 200g red cabbage
9. 30g fresh coriander or herb of choice
10. 1 medium aubergine

First soak 12 x 25cm wooden skewers to prevent them burning by putting them into a large bottle filled with water. Put the lid on, shake, then leave to soak for 5 minutes.

Meanwhile, put the peanut butter, coconut milk, tamari, maple syrup, lime juice and ginger into a large bowl, add 3 tablespoons of olive oil, and whisk together. Take 3 tablespoons of the sauce and set aside for the slaw.

To make the Asian slaw, grate the carrots and cabbage into a bowl and add a generous pinch of salt. Finely chop two-thirds of the coriander and add to the bowl. Add the reserved 3 tablespoons of sauce and stir to coat the veg. Taste and add salt and black pepper. Set aside while you make the skewers.

Slice the aubergine lengthways into ½cm slices (any thicker and they won't cook through), and mix well with the rest of the sauce, so that the aubergines are well coated.

Put the griddle pan or barbecue on to a medium heat to warm up while you thread the aubergines on to skewers.

We use 1 slice per skewer, making sure to spread out the slices well so that they are nearly flat, which will ensure they cook through. If you have some much shorter slices, you can add two to a skewer, making sure they are flat.

Spray a little oil on to the barbecue or griddle pan, then add the skewers in batches of 4 and cook for about 7–10 minutes on each side. The aubergine slices should be charred, soft and succulent when cooked.

Remove the aubergine skewers from the heat and drizzle over any leftover aubergine marinade and the rest of the coriander, finely chopped.

Serve with the slaw for a lovely zingy crunch.

AUBERGINE

Grilled Aubergine, Roasted Red Pepper and Lentil Salad

This is a wonderful centrepiece salad, packed full of colour and flavour. The combination of earthy lentils and sweet peppers with soft, grilled aubergines, contrasted with the pickled red onions, is so delicious! This is really easy to make, and grilled is always one of our favourite ways to eat aubergines.

10 INGREDIENTS

1. 2–3 aubergines (600g)
2. 30g flaked almonds
3. 1 small red onion, approx. 100g
4. juice of 1 lemon
5. 2 tbsp maple syrup
6. 2 x 400g tins of cooked lentils
7. 1 x 400g jar of roasted red peppers
8. 15g bunch of fresh mint or coriander
9. 1 pomegranate
10. 2 tsp balsamic vinegar

Slice the aubergines into ½cm-thick circles – you should get approx. 48 slices. Put them into a bowl and coat with 4 tablespoons of oil and a generous pinch of salt.

Heat a griddle pan on a high heat. Once hot, add the aubergines and cook on either side until they get soft and have some lovely char lines. You will have to do this in batches and it should take around 20 minutes. Alternatively, if you don't have a griddle pan you can fry them.

Put a non-stick frying pan on a medium heat and once it is hot add the flaked almonds. Cook for 3–4 minutes on each side until nice and brown, then remove from the heat and set aside for the garnish.

To pickle the red onion, peel and finely slice the red onion. Put into a glass or mug and add the lemon juice, a pinch of salt and 1 tablespoon of maple syrup. Mix well, then add water until the red onions are covered and leave to sit while you prepare the rest of the dish.

Drain and rinse the lentils. Remove the roasted red peppers from the jar and slice into smaller chunks. Remove the mint or coriander leaves from the stalks, or finely slice, including the stalks.

Deseed the pomegranate, keeping the seeds and making sure you remove all the white pith. The easiest way to do this is to hold the pomegranate with the crown facing up and cut across the centre – this exposes the seeds. Then hold it cut side down over a bowl and bang the back of the pomegranate with a wooden spoon until all the seeds pop out. Repeat with the other half. Remove any white pith from the seeds, as this is slightly bitter.

Mix the vinegar and the remaining 1 tablespoon of maple syrup in a bowl along with 4 tablespoons of oil and ½ teaspoon of salt.

Put everything except the flaked almonds into a large bowl and mix together. Taste and adjust the seasoning with more salt, ground black pepper or vinegar.

Decorate with the toasted flaked almonds and enjoy!

AUBERGINE

Chilli Peanut Aubergine Noodles

This is a quick and really flavourful noodle dish – the aubergine is cooked in a peanut sauce with the mushrooms to give it a softer, more meaty texture. Serve with your herb of choice and a sprinkle of toasted sesame seeds.

10 INGREDIENTS

1. 200g wholewheat noodles (or noodles of choice)

2. 1 large aubergine or 2 small

3. 200g mushrooms

4. 1 medium carrot

5. 5 tbsp tamari or soy sauce

6. 4 tbsp maple syrup

7. 3 tbsp apple cider vinegar

8. 4 tbsp peanut butter

9. ½ tsp chilli powder

10. 50g baby spinach

Cook the noodles in a pan of boiling water as per the instructions on the back of the packet, then drain and rinse.

Chop the aubergine and mushrooms into small bite-size pieces and grate the carrot. Put a large wide-bottomed pan on a high heat and leave to heat up. Add 2 tablespoons of olive oil and leave to heat up. Once hot, add the aubergine and mushrooms and cook for 8 minutes, stirring regularly. If they start to stick, add 2 tablespoons of water and, using your wooden spoon, 'deglaze' any caramelization from the bottom of the pan and incorporate.

Put the tamari, maple syrup, vinegar, peanut butter and chilli powder into a jug along with 6 tablespoons of water and ½ teaspoon of black pepper, and mix until smooth. Reduce the heat under the pan of aubergines and mushrooms to medium, then add half the sauce and cook for a further 4 minutes, stirring regularly.

Add the noodles, baby spinach, grated carrot and the remaining sauce to the pan and stir using a circular motion to mix and incorporate everything. Cook for 2 minutes.

Remove from the heat and adjust the seasoning to your liking. Add more chilli if you like it hot, and enjoy!

Layered Aubergine and Lentil Bake

Inspired by a traditional Greek moussaka, this is a favourite in our family. Dad often makes it – the aubergines melt in your mouth, and the earthy lentils complement the creamy sauce beautifully!

10 INGREDIENTS

1. 3–4 medium to large aubergines, about 1kg
2. 2 tbsp tamari or soy sauce
3. 1 onion
4. 3 cloves of garlic
5. 1 medium carrot
6. 1 x 400g tin of cooked lentils
7. 75g vegan Cheddar cheese
8. 1 x 400g tin of chopped tomatoes
9. 10 tbsp plain flour
10. 1 litre oat milk, or plant milk of choice

Preheat the oven to 200°C fan/220°C/gas 7. Line three baking trays with baking parchment.

Slice the aubergines into rounds approximately 1cm thick. You should get about 40–45 rounds. Put them into a bowl along with the tamari, add 3 tablespoons of oil and a pinch of salt, and mix well. Once covered, lay the slices of aubergine evenly in a single layer across the lined trays, then bake in the oven for 20 minutes.

While the aubergines are baking, peel and dice the onion and garlic. Cut the carrot in half lengthways and slice into thin rounds. Drain and rinse the lentils. Grate the vegan Cheddar.

Heat a non-stick frying pan on a high heat, and once hot add 1 tablespoon of oil along with the onion and carrot. Cook on a high heat for 5 minutes, stirring regularly, until the onions start to brown slightly. Add the diced garlic and cook for a further 1 minute until the garlic starts to go golden. Add 1 teaspoon salt and a small pinch of black pepper. Add the lentils and chopped tomatoes and bring to the boil, stirring regularly, then reduce to a simmer and leave for 5 minutes, stirring occasionally.

To make the béchamel sauce, put 9 tablespoons of olive oil into a pan on a medium heat. Once hot, sieve in the flour and cook for 1–2 minutes, stirring continuously with a whisk until it goes slightly golden. Slowly add the oat milk, stirring continuously. Bring to the boil, then reduce to a gentle simmer, stirring to be careful that nothing sticks to the bottom. Once simmering, and when it reaches a creamy texture, remove from the heat. Add a pinch each of salt and pepper, and mix in one-third of the vegan Cheddar, stirring it in as it melts. Taste and adjust the seasoning if it needs it, with salt, pepper or lemon juice.

Remove the baked aubergines from the oven. Using an ovenproof baking dish or lasagne dish approx. 32 x 22cm, add one-third of the béchamel, then cover that with a single layer of roasted aubergines. (If you have some smoked paprika, sprinkle a pinch over the aubergines.) Add a layer of the tomato lentil mixture, then cover that with another layer of roasted aubergines, followed by the remaining lentil mix. Cover with a final layer of aubergines, then add the rest of the béchamel, spread evenly across the top.

Scatter over the rest of the vegan Cheddar and bake in the oven for 8 minutes, or until golden. Serve with a simple green salad.

AUBERGINE

Aubergine Parmigiana

A rich tomato sauce, roasted aubergines and basil, all layered in one delicious mouth-watering experience! Here is our 10-ingredient version of the classic Italian dish, one of our mom's favourite meals. We love to serve this with a simple green salad and some garlic bread.

10 INGREDIENTS

1. 70g cashew nuts
2. 3 small aubergines (600g)
3. 1 head of garlic
4. 2 small onions, or 1 large
5. 60g sun-dried tomatoes (not in oil)
6. 2 x 500g jars of passata
7. 1 tbsp maple syrup
8. 50g fresh basil
9. juice of ½ a lemon
10. 1 tbsp nutritional yeast

Preheat the oven to 200°C fan/220°C/gas 7. Line two baking trays with baking parchment. Soak the cashew nuts in boiling water for 10 minutes while you prepare and cook the aubergines.

Slice the aubergines lengthways into ½cm-thick slices. Brush both sides of the aubergine slices with olive oil so that each slice gets an even coating, and transfer to the baking trays, ensuring they are spaced out as best you can. Sprinkle with a large pinch of salt and put into the oven for 20 minutes, until the slices start to turn golden and char. Chop the top off the head of garlic and place it in the oven directly on the middle rack to bake beside the tray of aubergines.

While the aubergines and garlic are baking, peel and finely chop the onions. Chop the sun-dried tomatoes.

Put a large wide-bottomed non-stick pan on a high heat and add 1 tablespoon of oil. Once hot, add the onion and a pinch of salt. Cook for 4–5 minutes, stirring regularly. Add the passata, maple syrup and sun-dried tomatoes and bring to the boil, then reduce to a gentle simmer. Add a large pinch of salt and black pepper. Remove the basil leaves from their stalks and set aside. Finely chop the stalks and add to the tomato sauce. Leave to further reduce on a low heat.

Take the garlic and aubergines out of the oven and leave to cool for a few minutes. Squeeze out the roasted garlic cloves, roughly chop and add to the tomato sauce. Remove the sauce from the heat and blend smooth with an immersion blender.

Drain the cashews and rinse in a colander, then place in a blender along with the lemon juice, nutritional yeast, 1 tablespoon of olive oil, a good pinch of salt and 3–4 tablespoons of water and blend until it reaches a super-smooth creamy texture.

In a large casserole dish (we use a 22 x 32cm dish), add a ladle of the rich tomato sauce to make a shallow layer. Top with a layer of baked aubergines and a few basil leaves. Now add another layer of tomato sauce, another layer of baked aubergines, a few more basil leaves, and repeat until you have used all the aubergine and tomato sauce.

Spoon the cashew cheese on top and roughly spread it out – we like it to be a bit patchy and not a complete covering, so that all the colours are visible. Put the dish into the oven and bake for 20 minutes, until the top starts to crisp up and the kitchen smells amazing.

AUBERGINE

Easy Aubergine, Butter Bean and Spinach Curry

This is a really tasty and easy curry that works perfectly as a mid-week dinner. Serve it with your grain of choice – we like to toast some wholemeal pitta breads and chop them into crunchy 'fingers' to dip in, too. Use low-fat coconut milk for fewer calories if you are so inclined.

10 INGREDIENTS

1. 1 large onion

2. 1 large aubergine

3. 1 x 400g tin of butter beans

4. 1 red chilli

5. 4 tbsp tamari or soy sauce

6. 1 x 400ml tin of coconut milk

7. 1 x 400g tin of chopped tomatoes

8. 1 tbsp curry powder

9. 100g fresh or frozen spinach

10. 1 lime

Peel and finely chop the onion. Cut the aubergine into small bite-size pieces – that way it will cook quicker. Drain and rinse the butter beans. Finely chop the chilli, removing the seeds if you don't like it spicy.

Put a large non-stick wide-bottomed pan on a high heat and add 1 tablespoon of oil. Once hot, add the onion and aubergine and cook for 5 minutes, stirring regularly. If they start to stick, add a couple of tablespoons of water, then, using your wooden spoon, 'deglaze' any of the caramelization from the bottom of the pan and incorporate. Mix 4 tablespoons of tamari with 4 tablespoons of water, reduce the heat to medium and pour half into the pan, cooking for about 2 minutes until it is all absorbed or evaporated. Repeat with the remaining tamari and water mix, stirring regularly. The aubergines should be soft and broken down at this stage and have a nice dark shiny colour to them – if not, simply cook them for a few minutes longer until they are lovely and soft.

Add the coconut milk, chopped tomatoes and curry powder and stir well. Bring to the boil, then reduce to a simmer. Add the butter beans and spinach and cook for a further 2 minutes.

Squeeze in the juice of half the lime. Taste and season with salt and pepper. Cut the remaining lime half into wedges. Serve in bowls and garnish each one with a sprinkle of chilli and a lime wedge.

Roasted Aubergine and Sweet Potato Curry Bake

Super-tasty and easy to make, this dish will leave you wanting more than one portion. Here we bake the curry to save you time. The crispy aubergine and sweet potato combo goes beautifully together. It makes a hearty winter dish but also tastes wonderful in summer too.

10 INGREDIENTS

1. 2 aubergines

2. 1 large leek

3. 2 red onions

4. 2 sweet potatoes

5. 3 tbsp tamari or soy sauce

6. 1 x 400ml tin of coconut milk

7. 400ml veg stock

8. 2 tbsp curry powder

9. 1 red chilli

10. a large bunch of fresh coriander

Preheat the oven to 200°C fan/220°C/gas 7. Line two baking trays with baking parchment.

Cut the aubergines into long wedge slices to give you about sixteen per aubergine. Chop the leek into large bite-size rounds, including the green parts, and give them a good wash. Peel the red onions and cut into quarters. Chop the sweet potatoes into bite-size pieces. In a cup mix the tamari with 4 tablespoons of oil.

Put the aubergines, leek and onions into a mixing bowl with the tamari mix. Add 1 teaspoon of salt and mix well, making sure all the aubergines are well coated.

Place all the aubergines, leek and onions on the lined baking trays, spacing them out so that they can bake well and crisp up and start to char. Put into the oven and bake for 30 minutes.

Put the coconut milk, veg stock and curry powder into a baking dish (32 x 22cm) and add the sweet potatoes. Finely chop the red chilli and add half of it to the dish, leaving the other half aside for garnish. Put the dish into the oven and bake for 30 minutes.

Take both trays and the dish out of the oven, then add the baked aubergine, leek and onion to the coconut, veg stock and sweet potato, and stir well.

Finely chop the coriander, including the stalks, and mix it through the dish. Garnish with the sliced chilli.

Baked Spiced Harissa Aubergine with a Chunky Salsa

Harissa is a spicy, salty, sweet chilli paste that originated in Tunisia and tastes delicious smeared over soft aubergine. We are confident that this simple dish will become one of your favourites for the sheer flavour. We make a chunky salsa to go on top, which adds a fresh lightness and vibrancy to this dish. Serve this with smashed baked potatoes (see page 254).

10 INGREDIENTS
1. 2 aubergines
2. 2 tbsp tamari or soy sauce
3. 3 red chillies
4. 8 sun-dried tomatoes (not in oil)
5. 40g almonds
6. 2 cloves of garlic
7. 1 avocado
8. 100g cherry tomatoes
9. 15g fresh coriander
10. ¼ of a red onion

Preheat the oven to 220°C fan/240°C/gas 9. Line two baking trays with baking parchment.

Cut the aubergines in half lengthways, then, using a knife, score the flesh side of each half lengthways and across the width, so that you create a chequerboard effect, being sure not to slice through the skin.

Sprinkle the parchment on one of the baking trays with salt. Place the aubergine halves on the parchment, flesh side up. The salt will help the aubergine skin to crisp up.

In a small bowl, mix 4 tablespoons of olive oil with the tamari. Using a pastry brush, spread the oil and tamari mix over the flesh of each aubergine half so that it goes into the cracks. Put the tray of aubergines into the oven and bake for 25 minutes.

To make the harissa, chop the tops off the chillies and cut in half lengthways, leaving the seeds in. Put them on the second baking tray and bake them in the oven for 10–15 minutes, until they start to char at the edges.

While the chillies are in the oven, soak the sun-dried tomatoes and almonds in boiling water and peel the garlic. Once the chillies are done, drain the sun-dried tomatoes and almonds and put them into a food processor with the chillies, peeled garlic, 4 tablespoons of oil, 2 tablespoons of water and a large pinch of salt. Blend until reasonably smooth – we like to leave a bit of texture. You may have to scrape down the sides once or twice to ensure it blends well.

Once the aubergines have been in the oven for 25 minutes, take them out. Smear the harissa paste on top, spreading it out so that there is a nice covering on each half, then put back into the oven to bake for a further 10 minutes. Keep any spare harissa, it makes a wonderful sandwich filler.

Cut the avocado in half, remove the stone, spoon out the flesh and slice into small cubes. Quarter the cherry tomatoes, finely chop the coriander, peel and finely dice the red onion, and put them all into a mixing bowl. Add 1 tablespoon of oil and a pinch of salt and mix well.

Remove the aubergines from the oven and serve with the chunky avocado salsa on top and any spare salsa on the side.

AUBERGINE

№. 2

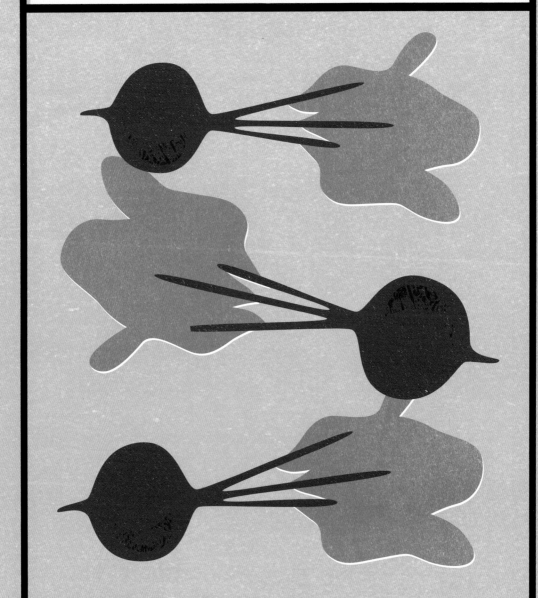

BEETROOT

Beetroot is one of the sweetest of all vegetables and is packed with nutrition. It can be roasted, baked, boiled, grated into salad, and used in cakes to add sweetness and its vibrant red colour.

Beetroot is one of the few veg you can eat every part of: the root, which is best known, the stalks, and the bright vibrant leaves, which are just like chard. After World War II, some veg became hard to get because of food rationing, so pickled beetroot became widespread across Europe and a staple in many households to make the fresh produce go further.

Much of the sugar in Ireland and the UK used to come from the sugar beet, which is a big white type of beetroot, from the same family but nutritionally totally different. Because of beetroot's natural sweetness, we have two desserts in this section. Beetroot goes particularly well with chocolate, as its earthiness can ground the sweet chocolate flavour, and we have created some epic beet brownies with a berry chocolate mousse (page 91) and a chocolate, coffee and beet cake (page 87). There is also a real diversity of savoury dishes, from a 10-ingredient version of one of our all-time most popular recipes, beetroot, walnut and feta burgers (page 83), to incredible vibrant and tasty beetroot pesto pasta with peas (page 81), to roasted warm beetroot hummus with toasted pitta breads (page 75), to show how versatile and incredibly tasty beetroot can be.

Beetroot is a root veg, closely related to turnip and swede. Beetroots come in a huge variety of colours and shapes, from red to white to golden to pink and even candy-striped. All beetroots are descendants of the sea beet, which grows wild along the coast of the Atlantic and the Mediterranean. In fact, beetroot was first cultivated for its leaves, and it took a long while for anyone to become hungry enough to eat the root and discover how tasty that part was too!

BUYING & STORING

If there are leaves on the beetroots you are buying, look for ones that look healthy and with firm stems, as these are great signs of freshness. We don't mind limp stems and droopy leaves, as long as the beetroot itself is still firm and fresh. Make sure the root is firm – if it is a little soft, just soak it in cold water for 30 minutes for it to firm up. Blemishes are easy to cut out.

The leaves will only last for a couple of days in the fridge and are best stored in an airtight container to keep the moisture in. The root will last for weeks in the fridge.

GROWING

Beetroot is in season for about ten months of the year, from June to March, and is really well suited to the UK and Irish climate, having few pests that eat it. It also keeps well, and is often stored in sand to retain its freshness during the hungry months when very little grows.

It's really easy to grow it from seed yourself. This year Steve's kids grew lots of beetroot from seed in the garden, and on top of having plenty of home-grown veg to eat, getting the kids involved in growing it meant they were much more interested in eating it! Steve's son Ned loved the bright vibrant leaves and beautiful shoots as it started to germinate and sprout within the first few weeks. We normally start to germinate beetroot seeds after St Patrick's Day, 17 March, which we often take as the start of spring, and plant the seedlings out in early April/May. They can be planted out even in late June. Plant them about 1cm deep and space them about 10–12cm apart, as they can grow up to 12cm in diameter. Like carrots and other root veg, they grow best in sandy rather than clay-like soil. Harvest beetroots when they are about the size of a tennis ball.

COOKING

When we were growing up, beetroot just meant pickled beetroot, and the strong acidic taste meant we hated it. Once we started the café we realized how easily grown it is and how it works in so many different ways, from salads, to mains, to desserts, always with that amazing vibrant colour.

Beetroot is widely available precooked and sold in vacuum packs, and this will work for many of the recipes in this section, though the colour will be duller and the flavour slightly pared back. In this chapter we have created recipes to show beetroot off in many different styles, from raw beetroot in a salad with orange, avocado and pumpkin seeds (page 78) to baked in the beet, sweet potato, feta and caramelized onion pastry parcels (page 77), and even in pink pancakes with raspberry compote and yoghurt (page 74) and one of our all-time favourites, roasted warm beet hummus with toasted pitta breads (page 75), which makes the perfect sharing platter.

NUTRITION

Beetroot is packed with antioxidants, evident from its bright red colour. When we first opened our juice bar, our aprons and hands used to be stained pink from juicing fresh beetroots. A simplistic way to think of antioxidants and their benefits for the body is that another name for rust is oxidation, so antioxidants help slow down the build-up of 'rust' in our body by slowing down cellular degradation. Studies have shown that it has helped improve athletic performance and stamina among professionals by as much as 2–3%. Not surprisingly, its bright red colour and the fact that it also bleeds are giveaway signs that it is great for our heart function and building healthy blood. It is also high in fibre, low in calories and about 88% water and great for digestion, among other things. The average beetroot weighs approximately 100g, so one beetroot is one of your 5-a-day.

BEETROOT

MAKES 7 medium (20cm) pancakes or 14 small (10cm)   **TAKES** 20 minutes

Pink Pancakes with Raspberry Compote and Yoghurt

Easy to make and a vibrant pink colour, these lovely fluffy American-style pancakes are a great breakfast, brunch or sweet lunch. Use wholemeal, brown or buckwheat flour for a healthier option.

8 INGREDIENTS

1. 100g uncooked beetroot
2. 1 orange
3. 220g self-raising flour
4. 300ml non-dairy milk of choice
5. ⅓ of a ripe banana
6. 3 tbsp maple syrup
7. 250g frozen or fresh raspberries
8. 200g coconut yoghurt

Wash the beetroot and remove any dirt and blemishes. Grate the beetroot into a mesh sieve over a bowl. Add a pinch of salt, mix with a spoon and leave to sit for 2 minutes. Then, using the same spoon, squeeze out as much juice as you can. Discard the pulp and keep the juice.

Zest the orange and squeeze the juice. Put the beet juice into a blender with half the orange zest, the flour, milk, banana, ½ teaspoon of salt, 1 tablespoon of maple syrup and 125g of the frozen raspberries. Blend until smooth.

Put the remaining raspberries into a saucepan on a medium heat and add the rest of the orange zest, the orange juice and the remaining 2 tablespoons of maple syrup. Put a lid on the pan and bring to the boil, then reduce to a simmer for 5 minutes with the lid ajar, leaving room for the steam to escape, stirring occasionally. Remove from the heat.

To cook the pancakes, heat a non-stick frying pan on a high heat. Once the pan is hot, reduce the heat to medium, then add 1 teaspoon of oil and enough batter to make a 10cm pancake – this is about 50ml of batter (double if making larger pancakes).

Cook until bubbles start to form and the edges start to dry out. Turn, using a small spatula, and cook the other side until it goes golden. Put your cooked pancake on a plate and keep warm by covering with a clean tea towel. Continue to make the rest of your pancakes until all the batter is used.

Serve each pancake with a generous dollop of coconut yoghurt, some of the raspberry compote and a drizzle of maple syrup, along with any remaining banana!

[handwritten notes: LO, 400/12, 15/1, 25/2, 75, 20/31, so margerine, beet only provide color, 655/46, OK for a pancake w/ no egg or oil – but a bother to get pink color]

MAKES approx. 500g of beet hummus　　**TAKES** 30 minutes

Roasted Warm Beet Hummus with Toasted Pitta Breads

This is as tasty as it looks! We roast raw beetroot here, but if you like you can use store-bought vac-packed beetroot – it won't be quite as vibrant a colour or as sweet, but will still work fine as a time-saving option. We like to garnish this with gomasio, black and white sesame seeds mixed with sea salt.

7 INGREDIENTS

1. 250g uncooked beetroot
2. 1 x 400g tin of chickpeas
3. 2 cloves of garlic
4. 2 tbsp light tahini
5. juice of 1 lemon
6. ½ tsp ground cumin
7. 6 wholemeal pitta breads

Preheat your oven to 180°C fan/200°C/gas 6.

Wash the beetroot and remove any dirt and blemishes, then roughly chop into bite-size pieces and put them on a baking tray. Sprinkle with a good pinch of salt and drizzle over 1 tablespoon of olive oil, then mix to make sure the beets are coated. Bake for 25 minutes, or until the beets are well roasted and slightly charred around the edges.

Meanwhile, drain and rinse the chickpeas. Put them into a pan of boiling water on a medium heat for 10 minutes to warm up, then drain.

Peel the garlic and put it into a food processor with the roasted beetroot, drained chickpeas, tahini, lemon juice, cumin, 1 teaspoon of salt, ½ teaspoon of black pepper, 4 tablespoons of water and 4 tablespoons of oil, and blend for about 2–3 minutes, until nice and smooth. Add a little more water if you think it needs it to reach your desired texture. Taste and season with salt and black pepper.

Toast the pitta breads and slice them into dipping 'fingers'.

Serve the hummus in a bowl on a large board with the toasted pitta breads, and enjoy!

BEETROOT

Beet, Sweet Potato, Feta and Caramelized Onion Pastry Parcels

Super-tasty, savoury, sweet, crispy pastry parcels, these are banging with flavour and work great with a simple salad. Beets are in season July to autumn and store well, so these can make a lovely Christmas party dish, or a light summer lunch.

8 INGREDIENTS

1. 300g uncooked beetroot
2. 300g sweet potatoes
3. 1 red onion
4. 2 tbsp balsamic vinegar
5. 1 sheet of vegan ready-rolled puff pastry (320g)
6. 100g vegan feta
7. a few sprigs of thyme
8. 2 tbsp oat milk, or non-dairy milk of choice

Preheat the oven to 180°C fan/200°C/gas 6. If using frozen puff pastry, ensure it is fully thawed.

Chop the beetroot and sweet potato into 1cm pieces. Peel and slice the onion. Put them all on a lined baking tray and drizzle over the balsamic vinegar, 1 teaspoon of salt and 2 tablespoons of olive oil and mix well. Bake in the oven for 30 minutes.

Remove the roasted veg from the oven and allow to cool for 5 minutes. Roll out the puff pastry on a lightly floured surface so it measures 32 x 42cm, then cut it into quarters. Line two trays with baking parchment. Transfer the pastry quarters to the two lined baking trays, ensuring that they are spaced well apart.

Cut the vegan feta into cubes and pick the thyme leaves off the stalks.

Spoon approximately a quarter of the veg into the middle of each of the 4 puff pastry rectangles, leaving around 5cm uncovered all the way around so you can seal your parcels. Add a quarter of the vegan feta to each and some of the thyme leaves.

Gather the sides of the pastry so that they overlap and seal the parcel by pinching together and twisting slightly in the centre, taking care not to tear the pastry. Brush the tops and sides of the pastry with oat milk.

Bake in the oven for 25 minutes, until the parcels are an even golden colour.

BEETROOT

SERVES 2 as a main, 4 as a side   **TAKES** 20 minutes

Beetroot, Orange, Avocado and Toasted Pumpkin Seed Salad

This vibrant salad makes a great lunch or side dish. Packed with flavour as well as antioxidants and nutrition, it is also very straightforward to make. It is best to dress only what you are going to eat, as the salad doesn't keep as long, once dressed. We remove the orange segments from their skins – it's a small step but it makes them melt in your mouth!

10 INGREDIENTS

1. 350g uncooked beetroot
2. 1–2 carrots
3. 35g pumpkin seeds
4. 35g sesame seeds
5. 2 ripe avocados
6. juice of ½ a lemon
7. 2 oranges
8. 3 tbsp balsamic vinegar or apple cider vinegar
9. 2 tbsp maple syrup
10. 50g baby spinach

Wash the beetroot and carrots and remove any dirt and blemishes, then top and tail them. Don't peel them, as most of the nutrition is in the skin. Grate them into a bowl.

Put a dry non-stick pan on a medium heat and toast the pumpkin and sesame seeds until they start to 'pop', colour and smell lovely, about 5–7 minutes.

Cut the avocados in half, remove the stones, spoon out the flesh and slice into small cubes. In a bowl, add the cubed avocado, lemon juice and a pinch of salt and mix well.

Using a small knife, cut the top and bottom off the orange so you have a flat surface to work with and then cut the peel off both oranges, making sure you remove the skin and the white pith underneath. Cut into each orange section on both sides and remove the segment, then repeat this until you have all the segments out. Squeeze the leftover orange pith over the grated beetroot and carrot so as not to waste any remaining juice, then discard the leftover fibre.

In a separate bowl, whisk together the vinegar, maple syrup, 4 tablespoons of olive oil, 2 teaspoons of salt and a pinch of black pepper. Pour this dressing over the grated beetroot and carrot. Add the baby spinach and half the toasted seeds and mix well to coat all the veg in the dressing.

Top the salad with the avocado and orange segments and the rest of the toasted seeds.

SERVES 4   **TAKES** 35 minutes

Beetroot Pesto Pasta with Peas

This started out as a simple idea to get vibrant pink-coated pasta, but ended up an incredibly beautiful dinner! Use your favourite pasta – wholemeal for a healthier version. Any spare pesto, just keep it for a sandwich spread, which will last for a week in the fridge. You can use ready-cooked beetroot, but the colour will be less vibrant.

7 INGREDIENTS

1. 200g uncooked beetroot

2. 400g dried wholemeal spaghetti or penne pasta

3. 130g pine nuts

4. 100g frozen peas

5. 1½ cloves of garlic

6. 2 tbsp balsamic vinegar

7. 30g rocket

Preheat your oven to 200°C fan/220°C/gas 7.

Wash the beetroot and remove any dirt and blemishes, then roughly chop into bite-size pieces and put them on a baking tray. Sprinkle with a good pinch of salt and drizzle with a little olive oil. Bake for 20–30 minutes, or until they are well roasted and slightly charred around the edges.

Bring a medium saucepan of water to the boil, then add 1 tablespoon of salt and the pasta and cook as per the packet instructions.

Put the pine nuts into a dry frying pan on a high heat and cook for 5 minutes, stirring regularly until golden. Remove from the heat and set aside.

Drain and rinse the pasta, keeping the pasta water. Put the peas into a bowl, pour over the pasta water and leave them to sit for 5 minutes. Then drain and rinse.

Peel and chop the garlic and put it into a food processor with the cooked beets, balsamic vinegar, 150ml of oil and 1 teaspoon of salt, then blend until smooth. Add the pine nuts and pulse so they are broken up, but still a little chunky to give some nice texture.

To bring the dish together, put the cooked pasta into a large pan and add half the beetroot pesto, half the peas and the rocket. Fold together and warm on a medium heat for 2–3 minutes, stirring regularly.

Divide between 4 bowls and serve with the remaining peas scattered on top.

BEETROOT

Beetroot, Walnut and Feta Burgers

These wonderful burgers are always popular in our café, so here is an easier version that still tastes fab. In this recipe we make a simple cashew feta that adds flavour and texture to the burgers. They go great served with your favourite hummus and a quick salad.

9 INGREDIENTS

1. 60g cashew nuts
2. 400g uncooked beetroot
3. 10 spring onions
4. 140g walnuts
5. 80g vegan Cheddar cheese
6. 20g fresh mint
7. juice of 1 lemon
8. 100g fresh breadcrumbs
9. 150g hummus of choice (e.g. carrot hummus, page 148)

Preheat the oven to 180°C fan/200°C/gas 6. Line two baking trays with baking parchment.

Put the cashew nuts into a bowl and cover with boiling water, then leave to soak for 10 minutes.

Wash the beetroot and remove any dirt and blemishes, then peel and grate into a bowl. Finely chop the spring onions. Roughly chop the walnuts and put them on one of the baking trays. Bake for 6–7 minutes, then remove and set aside.

Heat a non-stick frying pan on a medium heat. Once hot, add 1 tablespoon of olive oil along with the beetroot, spring onions and 1 teaspoon of salt, and cook for 4–5 minutes, stirring regularly. Remove and put into a large bowl to cool.

Grate the cheese and finely chop the mint leaves.

Drain and rinse the cashew nuts and put them into a food processor with 2 tablespoons of oil, half the lemon juice, ¼ teaspoon of salt and a pinch of black pepper. Blend until smooth, then add to the grated beetroot along with the cheese, walnuts, breadcrumbs, the rest of the lemon juice, the mint, ½ teaspoon of salt and ¼ teaspoon of black pepper and blend until the mixture just comes together, as we like to keep some nice texture to the burgers.

Divide the mixture into 4 even portions and shape into burgers. Place on the second lined baking tray and bake for 25 minutes. Remove and serve with hummus on top.

BEETROOT

Spaghetti and Beetballs

This delicious vegan take on spaghetti and meatballs is a quick and easy dinner for any day of the week. A great way to get veggies and wholefoods into a familiar family favourite. As an optional extra, serve with some vegan Parmesan to give another pop of flavour.

10 INGREDIENTS

1. 100g cashew nuts

2. 400g dried wholemeal spaghetti

3. 100g uncooked beetroot

4. 2 red onions

5. 4 small cloves of garlic

6. 1 x 400g tin of black beans

7. 100g fresh breadcrumbs

8. 1 tsp fennel seeds (optional)

9. 2 x 400g tins of chopped tomatoes

10. a few fresh basil leaves, to serve

Preheat the oven to 170°C fan/190°C/gas 5.

Spread the cashews on a baking tray and toast in the oven for 6–7 minutes. Set aside.

Bring a medium saucepan of water to the boil and add a generous pinch of salt. Add the spaghetti and cook as per the packet instructions, then drain, rinse, and put the pasta back into the same pan.

While the pasta is cooking, let's make our beetballs. Wash the beetroot and remove any dirt and blemishes, then coarsely grate it into a bowl. Peel and finely chop the onions and garlic. Drain and rinse the black beans.

Put a non-stick pan on a high heat. Add 1 tablespoon of oil and, once hot, add the onions and cook for 2–3 minutes, until they start to brown. Turn the heat down to medium, add the garlic and cook for a further 2 minutes. Remove half the garlic and onions and set aside to use later for the tomato sauce.

Add the grated beetroot to the onions and garlic in the pan, along with 1 teaspoon of salt and the drained black beans, and cook for 5 minutes. Remove from the heat, then transfer to a food processor with the breadcrumbs, toasted cashew nuts, and a pinch of black pepper, and blend until smooth.

Remove the mixture from the food processor and shape into 14–16 small smooth balls about the size of a lime. Flatten each ball slightly.

Put the same non-stick pan back on a high heat and add 1 tablespoon of oil. Once hot, add the fennel seeds and fry for 30 seconds, then add the reserved onion and garlic. Fry for another couple of minutes, then add the chopped tomatoes, 1 teaspoon of salt and a pinch of black pepper, and bring to the boil. Once boiling, reduce to a simmer and cook for 5–10 minutes, stirring occasionally. Add the tomato sauce to the cooked pasta, mix well, and set aside in a lidded pan to keep it warm while you cook the beetballs.

Put the same non-stick pan on a high heat and add 2 tablespoons of oil. Once hot, add the flattened beetballs and fry in batches until brown, about 2–3 minutes on each side. Remove from the heat.

Serve the spaghetti with 3 or 4 beetballs per person, with some basil leaves and grated vegan Parmesan scattered over.

Veggie Red Curry

This sweet red curry tastes and looks fantastic, as the beetroot gives it a really vibrant colour. It makes a lovely lunch or dinner – we devoured it a number of times in the garden as the weather got warmer. Serve this with brown rice or noodles of choice (we like to use wholewheat or brown rice noodles).

10 INGREDIENTS

1. 2 bunches of spring onions

2. 200g mushrooms

3. 1 medium sweet potato

4. 1 head of broccoli

5. 1 red chilli

6. 1 x 400g tin of chickpeas

7. 100g uncooked beetroot

8. 1 x 400ml tin of coconut milk

9. 4 tbsp tamari or soy sauce

10. 2 limes

Finely chop the spring onions and put a quarter of them aside for garnish. Finely chop the mushrooms, and chop the sweet potato and broccoli into small bite-size pieces, including the broccoli stalk. Finely slice the red chilli, removing the seeds and white membrane if you don't like it hot. Drain and rinse the chickpeas.

Wash the beetroot and remove any dirt and blemishes, then grate it, using a box grater. Put it into a sieve with a larger bowl underneath it, along with a generous pinch of salt, and mix well. Leave to sit for 2–3 minutes, then give it a squeeze using the back of a spoon until you get approx. 1 tablespoon of beetroot juice. Set any beetroot left in the sieve aside.

Heat 1 tablespoon of olive oil in a wide-bottomed non-stick pan on a high heat. Add the mushrooms and a pinch of salt and cook for 4–5 minutes, stirring regularly until they reduce right down and start to brown.

Add the sweet potato, chopped chilli, the remaining chopped spring onions and a good pinch of salt, then put a lid on the pan and cook for a further 4 minutes, stirring occasionally to prevent the veg sticking.

Add the broccoli and cook for a further 4 minutes with the lid on, stirring occasionally.

Add the coconut milk, tamari, chickpeas, 400ml of water and the zest of 1 lime and stir well. Then squeeze in the juice of the 2 limes and the beetroot juice, along with any grated beetroot from the sieve. Bring to the boil, then reduce to a simmer for a further 3 minutes. Taste and season with salt and black pepper.

Serve in bowls, garnished with the reserved spring onions.

Chocolate, Coffee and Beet Cake

The combination of coffee, beetroot and chocolate is a beautiful thing. The earthy beetroot, with the sweetness from the buttercream and the coffee, adds an amazingly subtle mocha flavour. This is an easy way to make a seriously impressive cake!

9 INGREDIENTS

1. 320g self-raising flour

2. 300g caster sugar

3. 80g cocoa powder

4. 200g cooked beetroot

5. 300ml strong black coffee

6. 1 tsp vanilla extract

7. 200g vegan unsalted block butter

8. 380g icing sugar

9. 4 tbsp cocoa powder

Preheat the oven to 180°C fan/200°C/gas 6. Grease two 20cm springform cake tins and line them with baking parchment on the base and sides.

In a large mixing bowl, sieve the flour, caster sugar and cocoa together and mix well. Make a well in the centre.

Cut the cooked beetroot into small pieces. Put the beetroot, coffee, 150ml of vegetable oil and the vanilla into a food processor and blend until all the beetroot is broken down and the texture is super-smooth.

Add the wet ingredients to the dry ingredients and mix well, using a spatula, until they just come together in a nice smooth uniform batter. Divide the mixture between the two lined cake tins and level the tops. Bake for 30 minutes, rotating the tins halfway through the cooking time to ensure they cook evenly.

While the cakes are baking, prepare the buttercream. Make sure the vegan block butter is at room temperature. Add the vegan block butter to a large bowl, and using a fork, cream the butter, then sift in the icing sugar and the cocoa powder. Using a fork or whisk, bring it all together. Alternatively, you can use an electric mixer or stand mixer, and but a fork will work fine too!

Check if the cakes are cooked by inserting a skewer into the centre. It should come out clean – if not, put back into the oven and cook a little longer. Remove the cakes from the oven and set aside on a rack to cool fully.

To assemble the cake, choose your base cake and place it on a plate. Gently spread half the buttercream evenly over this base cake, using a spatula, up to 1cm from the edge. Gently place the second cake on top, pressing it down lightly so the filling spreads and just comes to the edge. Add the rest of the buttercream to the top of the cake, working your way from the centre, spreading it to the edge.

Decorate as you like – we like to add raspberries to serve, and if you have a chocolate bar, slice it into thin shards and sprinkle them over the top.

Cut into big doorstopper slices!

BEETROOT

Beet Brownies with Berry Choc Mousse

Here we have a berry-infused chocolate mousse to top these wonderful beetroot brownies. They are really easy to make, and the beetroot adds a lovely earthiness that complements the sweet chocolate so well. These are a beautiful healthier treat!

9 INGREDIENTS

1. 200g cooked beetroot

2. 200g melted coconut oil

3. 200ml maple syrup

4. 1 tbsp vanilla extract

5. 100g ground almonds

6. 100g self-raising flour

7. 60g cocoa powder

8. 200g dark chocolate

9. 2 berry tea bags

Preheat the oven to 180°C fan/200°C/gas 6. Line a deep 28 x 18cm baking tray with baking parchment.

Chop the beetroot into small pieces, then put them into a food processor with the coconut oil, maple syrup and vanilla and blend until super-smooth.

Sieve the ground almonds, self-raising flour and cocoa powder into a large bowl. Add a pinch of salt and mix well. Make a well in the centre and pour in the wet ingredients. Fold until well combined.

Pour the batter into the lined tray and spread level. Bake for 20 minutes, rotating the tin halfway through to ensure it bakes evenly. Take out of the oven and leave to cool fully before adding the chocolate mousse.

Put equal parts of cold water and ice into a medium-sized metal bowl to make an ice bath. Set a smaller metal bowl inside, ensuring that the bottom of the bowl is touching the iced water.

Finely chop the dark chocolate. Pour 150ml of boiling water into a medium pan and add the 2 berry tea bags. Bring to the boil, then reduce to a simmer for 2 minutes. Remove the tea bags and turn off the heat, then add the chocolate to the pan of infused boiling water. Stir with a spatula or whisk until all the chocolate has melted and it resembles the texture and smoothness of a thick hot chocolate. Transfer this to the smaller metal bowl, and place this bowl into the larger one containing ice and water, ensuring none of the water gets in.

Whisk the chocolate mixture vigorously. Continue to whisk until the mixture has the consistency of softly whipped cream – the peaks should just hold their shape and it should take about 3–4 minutes. If it gets too thick don't worry, just add a little more boiling water and stir it in.

Spread the chocolate mousse generously on top of the cooled brownies, then cut to your desired size and enjoy!

BEETROOT

NO. 3

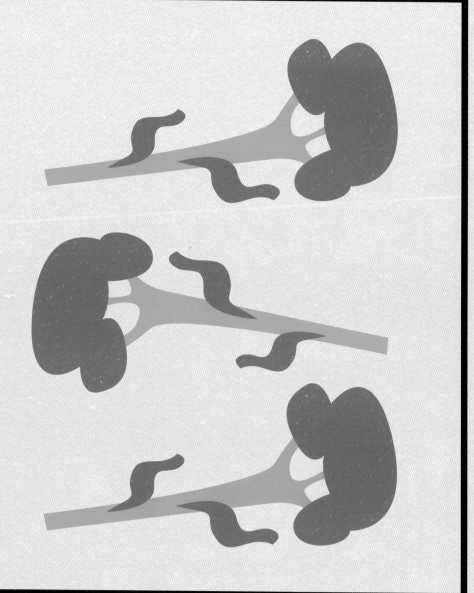

BROCCOLI

Broccoli is part of the brassica family and is closely related to cauliflower, cabbage and kale. It supposedly originated in Iraq and Syria, and it made its way to Italy via Cyprus. It was still referred to as 'Italian asparagus' as late as the eighteenth century. In fact, it gets its name from the Italian word for 'little branch' or 'little arm'.

It is a tough vegetable, and like kale and Brussels sprouts it comes into its own in winter with the cold and frost. The green bushy heads you see are flower buds that have started to grow and stopped – another thing broccoli has in common with cauliflower. There are three main types of broccoli: the most common is called calabrese – it's the one with the clustery head and thick stalk. Sprouting broccoli has long thin stems and comes in green or purple in winter. And, finally, tenderstem broccoli is somewhere in the middle, with a thin stem and a head on the end. Our favourite type is purple sprouting broccoli, a delicacy that rivals even asparagus. It is more winter-hardy and usually has more flavour than calabrese broccoli, and is delicious pan-fried with a little garlic and chilli.

We would often find broccoli stalks in baskets in the shop after customers had secretly cut them off with their keys, just taking the florets, but the stalk is actually packed full of fibre and goodness too. There are plenty of ways to use every bit of it, which we'll show you later. Broccoli pairs well with most savoury foods: we use it in our broccoli, roasted red pepper and feta calzones (page 99), char it in our sticky charred broccoli and tofu ribs (page 113) and serve it as the ultimate winter centrepiece meal in our creamy broccoli pie (page 111). Even just the stalks on their own work great in soup, as we show in the cream of broccoli and toasted hazelnut soup (page 106).

BUYING & STORING

Buy broccoli with a nice firm vibrant head – not limp, starting to flower or turning yellowish. When buying sprouting broccoli you don't want it to be droopy, so hold it upright and see that it stands strong and firm.

Broccoli needs to be stored in the fridge and likes a bit of moisture too – wrap it in a damp cloth for best results. Eat before it starts to turn soft.

GROWING

Broccoli is a cool-season crop that likes the sun, and is best grown in the colder weather of spring or autumn. It can be started in later winter or early spring for an early summer crop, or in mid to late summer for an autumn crop. The warm weather will affect the quality of the broccoli head, so the aim is to get broccoli to mature either before or after the peak of summer.

Sprouting broccoli is in season in winter, from January to May, when few other home-grown veg are ready to be harvested. The cold and frost help sweeten it and bring it to fruition. Normal broccoli (calabrese) and tenderstem are summer veg, in season from June to October and even November.

For years we have sprouted broccoli seeds on our sprout farm and sold them as part of a hero mix. Broccoli sprouts are widely known for their possible health benefits, such as helping circulation, improving asthma and other respiratory illnesses. Broccoli seeds can germinate in soil temperatures as low as 4°C, but will grow quicker in warmer soil temperatures. We normally germinate seeds indoors in spring, and plant them outside once the risk of frost is gone. Plant the seedlings 1–1.5cm deep and 30–50cm apart.

COOKING

We like to eat broccoli with a little bite to it, so we try to avoid overcooking. You can eat it raw in salads – just massage it with some lemon juice, a pinch of salt and a little oil as we do in the broccoli and kale 'Caesar' salad (page 97). Alternatively, you can lightly steam it, as we do in the chilli, broccoli and leek tacos (page 107), or stir-fry it, as in the sweet chilli broccoli noodle salad (page 103), or even bake it, as in the creamy broccoli and leek pasta bake (page 110).

Broccoli is a very versatile veg that adds colour and nutrition to most dishes. The stem, leaves and stalks are also edible – people often throw away the stalk, but it is wonderfully starchy in taste and goes well as the base for soups in place of celeriac or potato. It also works great when chopped finely and fried as the base for stews, casseroles and curries.

NUTRITION

Like most green veg, broccoli is high in vitamin C and in vitamin K, which helps with blood clotting. It is also high in fibre, so it benefits our gut health and therefore our immune system, as most of our immune system cells are based in our gut. It also contains decent amounts of protein. In terms of minerals, it is rich in iron and calcium, so it's great for healthy blood.

80g of broccoli is considered one of your 5-a-day, and the average serving size is 145g, which means it's easy to hit that target.

BROCCOLI

SERVES 3   **TAKES** 40 minutes

Broccoli and Kale 'Caesar' Salad

This is a delicious multifaceted salad, with the crunch of the baby gem, the crispy croutons, the salty capers, the smoky umami tempeh and the bite of the broccoli, all in a lovely creamy dressing. Capers are easy to find and are little salty, chewy bombs of flavour! Use store-bought vegan mayo and barbecue sauce to save yourself time.

9 INGREDIENTS

140 / 11%

1. 200g tempeh or firm tofu

2. 175g barbecue sauce (page 276)

3. 3–4 slices of sourdough bread *250*

4. 1 large head of broccoli *15*

5. juice of ½ a lemon

6. 100g any combination of kale, 1 head of cos or romaine lettuce

7. 2 baby gem lettuces

8. 80g capers in brine

9. 100g vegan mayo (page 275) *360*

Preheat the oven to 200°C fan/220°C/gas 7.

Slice the tempeh or firm tofu into thin strips, about 3mm thick. Put into a bowl, add the barbecue sauce and mix well. Pour out on to a baking tray and bake for 10 minutes. Then flip the tempeh/tofu and bake again for 15 minutes. Take from the oven and leave to cool.

Chop the slices of bread into approx. 2cm cubes and put them into a bowl with 3 tablespoons of oil, a generous pinch of salt and a pinch of black pepper. Spread them out on a second baking tray and bake for 8 minutes, then turn them and bake for a further 5 minutes. Take from the oven and leave to cool.

Chop the broccoli into small florets and discard the tough stalk (or you can keep this as a base for soup – it works well in the cream of broccoli and toasted hazelnut soup on page 106, for example). Place in a bowl with the lemon juice, a pinch of salt and 1 teaspoon of oil and massage the broccoli.

Cut the main rib out of the kale and tear the leaves up small. Cut the base off the baby gem lettuces to free the leaves, and peel off the leaves. Put the kale, broccoli and baby gem lettuce into a large salad bowl.

Remove the capers from their brine, keeping 15ml of the brine aside to use in the mayo dressing. Mix the mayo and the caper brine together along with ¼ teaspoon of black pepper. Drizzle the mayo dressing over the broccoli, baby gem and kale salad along with two-thirds of the capers, and mix so that each leaf is well coated. Top with the barbecue tempeh, the rest of the capers and the crispy croutons. Enjoy!

+765/11

Broccoli Pesto Pasta

This is a quick, easy, tasty way to get more greens into your day! The idea of broccoli pesto might sound strange, but trust us – this is a great way of hiding green veg and giving you a beautiful creamy pesto. Steve's kids loved this one! We like to serve it with wholemeal spaghetti or tagliatelle, but you can choose your favourite pasta.

6 INGREDIENTS

1. 200g broccoli
2. 1–2 cloves of garlic
3. 100g cashew nuts
4. 300g pasta of choice
5. juice of ½ a lemon
6. 1 red chilli (optional)

Cut the broccoli into small florets, and finely chop the stalk. Peel and chop the garlic. Fill and boil the kettle.

Put a frying pan on a medium heat. Once hot, add the cashew nuts and toast for 5–6 minutes, stirring regularly until they start to turn golden all over. Remove from the pan and set aside.

Put the pasta, broccoli and a generous pinch of salt into a large saucepan and cover with the boiling water. Bring to the boil and cook according to the instructions on the packet. Drain, keeping a mug of the pasta water. Rinse the pasta and broccoli in cold water to stop the broccoli cooking and to wash away some of the pasta starch.

Put the broccoli florets and stalks into a food processor or blender along with the toasted cashew nuts, lemon juice, garlic, 100ml of olive oil, 50ml of pasta water, ¾ teaspoon of salt and a pinch of black pepper. Blend until smooth. Taste and adjust the pesto to your liking by adding more salt or lemon juice.

Slice the red chilli. Put the frying pan back on a high heat and add the cooked pasta along with the pesto and 2 tablespoons of the pasta water. Mix together for 2 minutes, until well coated.

Serve the pasta in bowls with the red chilli sprinkled on top (leave the chilli out if you don't like spicy food).

Broccoli, Roasted Red Pepper and Feta Calzones

These are really tasty and make a great warm dinner or a lunch on the go. Calzones always sounded so fancy to us, growing up in Ireland – pasta was exotic, pizza was a treat and calzones were posh! A calzone is just a folded-over pizza that is super-gooey and delicious inside – here we make a delicious vegan feta cheese.

10 INGREDIENTS

1. 250g self-raising flour
2. 175g broccoli
3. 20g cashew nuts
4. 100g firm tofu
5. juice of ½ a lemon
6. ⅓ tsp garlic powder
7. 1 tbsp nutritional yeast
8. 80g roasted red peppers, from a jar
9. 4 tbsp pesto of choice
10. 4 tbsp tomato purée

Preheat the oven to 220°C fan/240°C/gas 9. Line two baking trays with baking parchment.

Put the flour into a mixing bowl and add 150ml of water and a good pinch of salt. Mix together to make a rough dough. Transfer it to a lightly floured surface and knead for 5 minutes until it is smooth and elastic. Alternatively, you could use a stand mixer with a dough hook and mix for 2–3 minutes. Divide the dough into 4 even balls and place them under an upturned bowl to rest while you make the filling.

Cut the broccoli into bite-size florets and finely chop the stalk. Bring a saucepan of water to the boil, add the cashew nuts and broccoli and simmer for 6–7 minutes. Using a slotted spoon or a large fork, carefully remove the broccoli and rinse under cold water to stop it cooking. Continue to simmer the cashew nuts for 5 minutes more. Drain, and give them a good rinse.

To make the vegan feta, put the cashew nuts into a food processor and crumble in the tofu. Add 60ml of olive oil, 1 teaspoon of salt, the lemon juice, garlic powder and nutritional yeast. Blend until smooth.

Lightly flour a rolling pin and your worktop and roll out the dough into thin circular shapes, about 20cm in diameter. Transfer the circles of dough to the two lined baking trays, ensuring they are spread out and not touching.

Drain and finely slice the red peppers. Mix the pesto and tomato purée together and generously cover the dough circles, leaving 1cm round the edge free from sauce. Scatter the broccoli, red pepper and feta across the top half of each circle, leaving the other half with just sauce.

Fold over the unfilled side of each dough circle or calzone, then crimp around the edges to seal. Finally, before baking, brush each calzone with ½ teaspoon of oil, to help it go golden in the oven.

Bake in the oven for 15 minutes, until golden. Serve piping hot with a green salad for a delicious lunch or dinner.

SERVES 2–3   **TAKES** 15 minutes

Sweet Chilli Broccoli Noodle Salad

This makes a lovely quick dinner or a cold salad. It's hearty, savoury and sweet. We used rice noodles, but you can use your favourite noodles – wholemeal or brown rice ones will be higher in fibre and healthier than white.

10 INGREDIENTS

1. 500g broccoli

2. 200g noodles of choice

3. 1 medium red pepper

4. 1 bunch of spring onions

5. 4 tbsp tamari

6. 1 tbsp paprika

7. ½ tsp chilli powder or cayenne pepper

8. 3 tbsp maple syrup

9. juice of 1 lime

10. 4 tbsp sesame seeds

Chop the broccoli into bite-size florets, keeping the stalk as a base for soup (it works well in the cream of broccoli and toasted hazelnut soup, see page 106).

Put a pan of boiling water on a high heat and add the noodles and the broccoli florets. Cook the noodles as per the instructions on the packet. Drain and rinse the noodles and broccoli once they are cooked.

Finely chop the red pepper, discarding the seeds and pith in the centre. Chop the spring onions at a 45-degree angle.

Mix the tamari, paprika, chilli powder, maple syrup and lime juice in a bowl and add a good pinch of black pepper.

Heat 2 tablespoons of olive oil in a large non-stick pan on a high heat. Once hot, add the chopped spring onions and red pepper and cook for 4–5 minutes, stirring regularly. Add the cooked broccoli, the noodles, the dressing and half the sesame seeds, and heat through for 3–4 minutes, stirring regularly.

Divide between two or three bowls and top with the rest of the sesame seeds. Garnish with more chilli powder, if you like it spicier.

BROCCOLI

103

Broccoli and Potato Cakes with a Chilli Mayo

This is a great way to use up any leftover mashed potato from a dinner the night before. At Christmas time we always have lots of mashed potato left over, and this is what we do with it. Try to use a floury potato such as Maris Piper or Queen, if possible.

9 INGREDIENTS

1. 1 x 300g head of broccoli
2. 500g potatoes
3. 2 onions
4. 2 cloves of garlic
5. 140g plain white flour
6. 100ml oat milk or non-dairy milk of choice
7. 8 tbsp sesame seeds
8. 1¼ tsp chilli powder
9. 100ml vegan mayo (page 275)

Chop the broccoli into bite-size florets and finely chop the stalk. Peel and roughly chop the potatoes, and peel and finely chop the onions and garlic. Put the broccoli florets into a food processor and pulse until finely chopped.

Put a pan of boiling water on a medium heat and add the potatoes and the finely chopped broccoli stalks. Cook for 10–15 minutes, until soft. Drain the potatoes and broccoli, and put them back into the still-warm pot. Leave to cool for 5 minutes, so any excess moisture can evaporate. Mash to break up the potato, then set aside to cool.

While the potatoes and broccoli are cooling, heat 1 tablespoon of olive oil in a wide-bottomed non-stick pan on a high heat. Once hot, add the onion and chopped broccoli florets along with ½ teaspoon of salt and cook for 5–10 minutes, stirring regularly. Turn the heat down to medium and add the garlic. Cook for a further 2 minutes, until the onions start to turn translucent and the mix begins to smell delicious!

Put the mashed potato, onion and broccoli mixture into a large mixing bowl, along with 100g of the flour, 1½ teaspoons of salt and 1 teaspoon of black pepper. Mix everything well, tasting and adjusting the seasoning. Shape the mixture into burger-shaped patties, about 80g each.

Put the remaining 40g of flour, the oat milk and sesame seeds into three separate bowls. Dip each potato cake in the flour first, coating it well, then into the oat milk and finally into the sesame seeds, giving them an even sprinkling on both sides. Reshape so each one is a nice smooth potato-cake shape.

Wipe out the wide non-stick pan, put it back on a medium heat, and add 2 tablespoons of oil. Once hot, add 3 potato cakes to the pan and cook on both sides for 4–5 minutes, until they start to turn golden. You need to be careful not to burn them, so keep checking. Repeat with the rest of the potato cakes until they are all cooked.

Mix the chilli powder through the vegan mayo and either serve as a dip for the potato cakes or drizzle over the top.

Cream of Broccoli and Toasted Hazelnut Soup

A creamy smooth and silky soup garnished with chunks of toasted hazelnut! The creaminess comes from the cashew-nut base and adds a lovely indulgent quality. This is a great recipe for using up any leftover broccoli stalks. You can simply use broccoli stalks on their own for this recipe, or a mixture of floret and stalk.

9 INGREDIENTS

1. 100g raw cashews
2. 500g broccoli or broccoli stalks
3. 2 onions
4. 3 cloves of garlic
5. 500g celeriac or potatoes
6. 1 litre veg stock
7. 1 litre oat milk or non-dairy milk of choice
8. 50g hazelnuts
9. 4 tbsp coconut yoghurt, to garnish

Put the cashews into a bowl, cover with boiling water and leave for 10 minutes, then drain.

Chop the broccoli roughly. Peel and slice the onions and garlic. Chop the celeriac or potatoes into bite-size pieces. The soup is going to be blended smooth, so there's no need to be too perfect with your chopping.

Put a large pan on a high heat. Add 1 tablespoon of olive oil and the onions. Cook for 3–4 minutes, stirring occasionally. Add the garlic and cook for a further 1 minute, stirring regularly. Add the celeriac or potatoes, broccoli and 1 teaspoon of salt. Cook for a further 3 minutes.

Turn the heat down to medium, put the lid on and leave the veg to cook in their own juices for 8–10 minutes, stirring occasionally, until the potato is cooked through. If the veg is sticking to the bottom of the pan, add a few tablespoons of veg stock.

Add the rest of the veg stock, with the oat milk and cashew nuts. Turn the heat up high and bring to the boil. Once boiling, reduce the heat to low–medium and cook for a further couple of minutes.

While the soup is simmering, put a dry pan on a medium heat and add the hazelnuts. Toast them for about 5–7 minutes, until they start to turn golden and the room begins to smell of roasting hazelnuts. Transfer the hazelnuts to a clean kitchen towel and fold over to cover. Rub the nuts in the towel first to remove any skins, then separate the skins from the nuts and discard the skins. Then, using a mug, crush and crumble the hazelnuts.

Remove the soup from the heat, add 1 teaspoon of salt and ½ teaspoon of black pepper, and blend smooth using an immersion blender. Taste and season with more salt and black pepper, if you think it needs it.

Serve in bowls, garnished with a splash of coconut yoghurt and the toasted hazelnuts sprinkled over.

Chilli Broccoli and Leek Tacos

This is a great sharing dish for the whole family and is packed with flavour. We like to let everyone build their own at the table – our kids love any dinner with guacamole and toasted wraps.

10 INGREDIENTS

1. 200g tenderstem broccoli or regular broccoli

2. 1 medium leek

3. 1 red chilli

4. 3 cloves of garlic

5. 200g cherry tomatoes (ideally different colours)

6. 1 x 400g tin of kidney or black beans

7. 1 bunch of fresh coriander (20g)

8. 3 ripe avocados

9. juice of 3 limes

10. 1 pack of small tortilla wraps (6–8 wraps)

If using regular broccoli, chop the florets from the stalk and slice them into small bite-size pieces; if using tenderstem broccoli, cut into thirds. Chop the leek, including the green parts, into approx. 2cm chunks and give them a good wash, then chop each piece in half lengthways. Finely slice the red chilli, leaving the seeds in if you like it hot. Peel and finely chop the garlic. Chop the cherry tomatoes in half. Drain and rinse the beans. Finely chop the coriander.

Heat 1 tablespoon of olive oil in a wide-bottomed non-stick pan on a high heat. Once hot, add the leek, chilli and a pinch of salt and cook for 3 minutes, stirring regularly.

Turn the heat down to medium–low and add the broccoli. Put a lid on the pan and cook the veg in their own juices for 5–6 minutes, stirring occasionally. Remove the broccoli and leek mixture from the pan and set aside.

Meanwhile, prep your guacamole. Cut the avocados in half, remove the stones, spoon out the flesh and slice into small chunks. Put the avocado chunks into a large bowl and add 1 teaspoon of salt, ½ teaspoon of black pepper, the juice of 2 limes, half the cherry tomatoes, half the chopped garlic and half the chopped fresh coriander. Using a fork, mash everything together and set aside.

Put the beans into the empty pan with the remaining garlic and cherry tomatoes, a good pinch of salt, ½ teaspoon of black pepper and the juice of 1 lime. Cook for 4–5 minutes, stirring regularly. Use the back of a wooden spoon to mash the beans. Add the remaining chopped coriander and mix through.

Put a small frying pan on a high heat and toast each tortilla wrap, so that it crisps up and starts to brown.

Serve the broccoli, mashed beans and guacamole in separate bowls in the middle of the table and let everyone make their own tortillas.

BROCCOLI

Creamy Broccoli and Leek Pasta Bake

This tasty, creamy, heart-warming pasta bake with a Mornay sauce makes a great comforting centrepiece dinner. Serve with toasted garlic bread and a simple side salad for a very satisfying meal.

10 INGREDIENTS

1. 400g wholewheat pasta
2. 3 cloves of garlic
3. 400g broccoli
4. 2 leeks
5. 100g vegan cheese
6. 50g baby spinach
7. 10 tbsp plain white flour
8. 1 litre oat milk or non-dairy milk of choice
9. 50g fresh breadcrumbs
10. 30g pine nuts

Preheat the oven to 180°C fan/200°C/gas 6.

Cook the pasta in a large pot of salted boiling water as per the instructions on the back of the packet.

Peel and finely chop the garlic. Cut the broccoli into florets and chop the stalks into small pieces. Chop the leeks, including the green parts, into approx. 2cm chunks and give them a good wash. Grate the vegan cheese.

Put a wide-bottomed non-stick pan on a high heat and add 1 tablespoon of olive oil, along with the broccoli, leeks and 1 teaspoon of salt. Cook for 3–4 minutes, stirring regularly.

Reduce the heat to medium–low, then put a lid on the pan and allow the veg to cook in their own juices for about 6–8 minutes, stirring occasionally. Remove the lid and add the garlic and baby spinach and cook for 1–2 minutes. Remove from the heat and mix through, then leave the lid off and allow the spinach to reduce and cook in the residual heat.

While the broccoli and leeks are cooking, make the sauce. Put a non-stick pan on a high heat and add 9 tablespoons of olive oil. Once hot, sieve the flour into the oil and whisk continuously for 2 minutes until golden. Slowly add the oat milk to the flour/oil mixture, whisking continuously. Add 1 teaspoon of salt and ¾ teaspoon of black pepper, along with half the grated vegan cheese. Bring to the boil, then reduce to a simmer, being careful that nothing sticks to the bottom. Once it has become a nice creamy sauce, remove from the heat, taste and season to your liking.

In a large ovenproof casserole dish, approx. 30 x 24cm, mix the pasta, sauce and cooked veg mixture well, making sure to level out the top.

In a separate bowl, mix the breadcrumbs, pine nuts and the remaining vegan cheese, and scatter over the top of the pasta bake. Pop into the oven for 20 minutes, or until the sauce is bubbling and the crumb top is golden brown. Serve straight from the oven for a lovely sharing, comforting meal!

SERVES 4–6   **TAKES** 1 hour and 20 minutes

Creamy Broccoli Pie

Crispy and creamy, with chunks of broccoli and an undercurrent of lemon and mustard. To make this recipe gluten-free, simply use gluten-free puff pastry, which is available in most supermarkets, and use gluten-free white flour for the béchamel sauce.

10 INGREDIENTS

1. 2 x 320g sheets of vegan ready-rolled puff pastry

2. 2 medium leeks

3. 400g celeriac, potatoes or parsnips

4. 1 x 400g broccoli head

5. 6 tbsp plain white flour

6. 700ml oat milk or non-dairy milk of choice, plus extra for brushing

7. 1 tsp garlic powder

8. 1 bay leaf

9. juice and zest of ½ a lemon

10. 1 tbsp Dijon mustard

Preheat your oven to 200°C fan/220°C/gas 7.

Grease your pie dish (20 x 20cm) with ½ tablespoon of oil so that the pastry doesn't stick. Place 1 sheet of pastry in the dish, ensuring it comes up the edges and slightly over the sides so it won't fall back down when it bakes. Cover with baking parchment and weigh it down with dried beans (approx. 200g). Bake for 15 minutes, then take it out of the oven, remove the baking parchment and beans, and set aside to cool.

Chop the leeks, including the green parts, into approx. 2cm chunks and give them a good wash. Peel the celeriac, potatoes or parsnips and chop into 1cm pieces. Chop the broccoli florets and stalk into 1cm pieces.

Put a large pan on a high heat and add ½ tablespoon of oil. Add the chopped leeks and a generous pinch of salt and cook for 4 minutes, stirring occasionally. Add the chopped celeriac, potatoes or parsnips and another pinch of salt. Stir well and turn the heat down to medium. Put the lid on and leave to sweat for 10–15 minutes, stirring occasionally, until the veg are tender. Add the broccoli and cook for a further 5 minutes.

To make the béchamel sauce, put 6 tablespoons of olive oil into a pan on a medium heat. Once hot, sieve in the flour and cook for 1–2 minutes, stirring continuously with a whisk until it goes slightly golden. Slowly add the oat milk, stirring continuously. Bring to the boil, then reduce to a gentle simmer, stirring to be careful that nothing sticks to the bottom. Once simmering, and when it reaches a creamy texture, remove from the heat. Add the garlic powder, the bay leaf and a pinch each of salt and pepper, and mix. Stir in the lemon zest and juice and the Dijon mustard. Taste and adjust the seasoning if it needs it.

Add the béchamel to the cooked leek, broccoli and celeriac mixture, and mix well. Taste and add more salt and pepper, if required. Leave to cool for 10 minutes.

Spoon the sauce into the blind-baked pie case until it comes almost to the top. Cut the remaining sheet of pastry to fit the top of the pie dish and make a small hole in the centre (this will allow excess moisture out of the pie). Working quickly, as the filling is warm, put the pastry lid on and use a fork to join the two sheets of pastry at the edges by compressing around the sides.

Using a pastry brush, brush the top of the pastry with oat milk. Bake in the oven for 15–20 minutes, until the pastry is nice and golden.

BROCCOLI

Sticky Charred Broccoli and Tofu Ribs

Charring broccoli really adds another dimension to this wonderful green vegetable, and served with a drizzle of glaze and these grizzly tofu ribs it's magnificent. The 5-spice is well worth sourcing, as it really adds a subtle extra dimension of flavour to this, but if you can't find it the ribs will still taste fab without it.

8 INGREDIENTS

1. 250g cooked rice or quinoa
2. 200g firm tofu
3. 200g broccoli
4. 3 tbsp maple syrup
5. 2 tbsp tamari or soy sauce
6. 2 tbsp tomato purée
7. 1 tsp Chinese 5-spice
8. 100g sauerkraut

Preheat the oven* to 220°C fan/240°C/gas 9. Line a baking tray with baking parchment.

Cook the rice or quinoa according to the instructions on the packet.

Slice the tofu into 2 rectangular pieces that are 1cm in thickness, then cut them across into triangles. Put them on the baking tray, brush with ½ tablespoon of oil, and bake for 15–20 minutes, until crispy on the outside.

Cut the broccoli into long thin bite-sized florets. Put them into a pan of boiling water and add a generous pinch of salt. Bring back to the boil, then reduce to a simmer and cook for 3–4 minutes. Drain and rinse in cold water to stop the broccoli cooking further.

In a cup, mix the maple syrup, tamari, tomato purée and 5-spice with 2 tablespoons of water to make a marinade.

Once the tofu is cooked, put three-quarters of the marinade into a wide-bottomed saucepan on a low heat and bring to the boil, stirring continuously. Once boiling, add the crispy tofu and cook for 1 minute, ensuring each triangle is well coated in the marinade. Take off the heat.

In a bowl, mix the broccoli with 1 tablespoon of olive oil. Put a griddle or frying pan on a high heat. Once hot, add the broccoli and cook until it has char marks on each side. Remove from the heat to a plate and drizzle over the rest of the marinade.

Spoon the cooked rice or quinoa into the middle of both the serving bowls and divide the charred broccoli and the sauerkraut between them. Finally, add the tofu.

*If you have an air fryer, you can cook the tofu for 15 minutes, upright, so the air can really circulate, to maximize the crispiness, instead of using an oven.

BROCCOLI

№. 4

CABBAGE

We decided to group cabbage and kale together, since they are both part of the brassica family, even though kale has become the more fashionable of the two and has greatly outranked cabbage in terms of popularity in recent years.

Both are closely related to broccoli, cauliflower and Brussels sprouts, and they are extremely nutritious green, leafy vegetables with multiple different varieties and uses. They are packed with goodness but in the past we struggled to eat enough of them, primarily because we didn't know what to do with them. Now we've learned how beautifully they can be cooked we'll have them in anything, even smoothies and salads, and every time we eat kale or cabbage we feel we are doing ourselves good.

Cabbage has a dense head and generally comes in three types: **white/red or Dutch cabbage** is the round cabbage, almost football-shaped, best known for its use in coleslaw or being fermented for sauerkraut. **Savoy cabbage** has big, beautiful leaves and is the classical image of a cabbage. It is dark green in colour with a round centre, ornate leaves and a mild flavour. **York cabbage** is a leafy green cabbage with a pointed shape that is strong in its flavour.

Similarly there are three main varieties of kale widely available: **curly kale** is the most common, and in Ireland it traditionally was used for colcannon. **Cavolo nero** or dinosaur kale has big long bubbly leaves with a central stem. It has a dark colour, hence it is sometimes known as black kale. **Red Russian kale** has vibrant reddish-purple stems with flat green leaves and almost looks like a kale version of rainbow chard. It is often softer and smaller in size than the other two, and you can find it in salad mixes.

Kale typically tastes milder than regular cabbage, and young black kale leaves from cavolo nero/dinosaur kale have a milder flavour than mature leaves of curly kale. You will see young kale leaves often used in salads now, as they have a very mild neutral taste to them and are much more nutritious than regular salad leaves.

CABBAGE

BUYING & STORING

When we first started the shop we were amazed how the older ladies would come in and go straight to the cabbage section, and proceed to give them all a good feel – they were looking for a cabbage with a strong heart or firm centre as a sign it was fresh.

Kale and cabbage are both best stored in the fridge in airtight containers or plastic bags, to keep in the moisture. Kale generally loses its freshness faster than cabbage. Kale and cabbage can often be pretty hardy – as a general rule, the leafier it is, the more likely it is to wilt. Both kale and cabbage can also be frozen.

Kale is on the dirty dozen list, compiled by the Environmental Working Group (EWG) each year to identify fruits and vegetables that have elevated levels of pesticides that may be concerning. So it is best to buy these veg, including kale, organically, wherever possible.

GROWING

Kale and cabbage are hardy winter vegetables and grow really well in the UK and Ireland. They are available all year round, but they are best September to February. White/red cabbages are stored for long periods, so are generally available also all year round. Traditionally they were fermented to make sauerkraut, as a way to preserve the cabbage so that it would last through the winter period. Steve's wife is Polish, and when he goes to Poland there is always a huge barrel of sauerkraut fermenting in the basement, which is eaten throughout the year. As with almost all veg, China is the biggest producer, and in fact they grew 48% of the world's cabbage in 2018.

COOKING

To prep kale, always remove the leaves and trim away the tough centre stalk, then tear or slice the leaves into smaller pieces. White and red cabbage are a little different – these are typically finely chopped or sliced in a food processor, as they are less leafy and much firmer.

We have a selection of cooked and raw kale and cabbage recipes here, from immunity boost kale smoothie (page 118), to Middle Eastern-style cabbage salad (page 122), to one of our favourites, Asian-style miso-glazed cabbage (page 126), to our family-pleasing red ricotta and kale pasta bake (page 135) – along with lots more to get you eating and enjoying more cabbage and kale!

NUTRITION

Cabbage is packed with fibre, which greatly improves gut health, and vitamin C (red cabbage has 30% more than white cabbage, due to its vibrant colour), as well as being a brilliant anti-inflammatory food. This means in a nutshell that it encourages our bodies to work at their optimum. Cabbage is also high in vitamin K, which helps with blood-clotting. Cabbage juice has been shown to promote the healing of stomach ulcers and many other stomach problems.

Kale is a modern-day celebrity vegetable of sorts, having undergone mass adoption following research heralding it as being the healthiest food, pound for pound, that exists. Kale is packed with fibre, antioxidants, vitamin C (containing 4½ times more than spinach), and it is also one of the world's highest sources of vitamin K, with about 60g of kale having more than seven times your daily RDA, as well as many minerals, including calcium, that most people don't get enough of.

The average cabbage weighs about 900g, so one-tenth of a cabbage is considered one of your 5-a-day. Similarly, 80g of kale is considered one of your 5-a-day.

SERVES 2 **TAKES** 5 minutes

Immunity Boost Kale Smoothie

Green, sweet, substantial: three words that don't often go together! This smoothie is a powerful way to start your morning. The ginger will put a pep in your step, the avocado, kale and almond butter will ensure your energy is consistent during the morning, and the dates will bring sweet deliciousness! Smash the remaining half avocado on to some toast with some salt and chilli for a lovely accompaniment.

8 INGREDIENTS

1. 50g kale

2. 12g ginger

3. 2 whole oranges

4. 8 Medjool dates

5. ½ a ripe avocado

6. juice of 1 lime

7. 2 tbsp almond butter

8. 275g iced or cold water

Chop the main ribs out of the kale, leaving just the leaves.

Peel the ginger (if using non-organic – if we are using organic ginger we like to leave the skin on). Peel the oranges and remove any pips. De-pit the dates, ensuring there are no stones left in. Remove the stone from the avocado half and scoop out the flesh.

Put all the ingredients into a blender and blend until smooth. Taste and add a little more water if it's too thick. We love to serve this with some ice for a refreshing, cool summer breakfast.

Hearty Cabbage, Sausage and Lentil Stew

A wholesome no-nonsense one-pan stew that is deeply nourishing and great family fare – the vegan sausages add a lovely bite that complements the earthy notes from the cabbage and lentils.

10 INGREDIENTS

1. 2 red onions

2. 3 cloves of garlic

3. 2 x 400g tins of cooked lentils

4. 4 vegan sausages

5. 250–300g Savoy or York cabbage

6. 2 x 400g tins of chopped tomatoes

7. 50g tomato purée

8. ½ tsp smoked paprika

9. 2½ tbsp tamari or soy sauce

10. 1 decent bunch of fresh coriander or fresh herb of choice

Peel and finely chop the onions and the garlic. Drain and rinse the lentils. Chop the sausages into bite-size pieces. Chop the cabbage, removing the tough centre stalks and finely slicing the leaves into strips. Finely chop the stalks as well – they will break down once cooked.

Heat 1 tablespoon of oil in a wide-bottomed non-stick pan on a medium heat. Once hot, add the onions and the sausages and cook for about 7 minutes, stirring regularly.

Once the sausages have started to brown and the onions are softening, add the cabbage and a pinch of salt and cook for a further 5 minutes, stirring regularly. Then add the garlic and cook for a further minute or two.

Add all the remaining ingredients (except the coriander) along with 1 teaspoon of salt and ½ teaspoon of black pepper and bring to the boil, then reduce to a gentle simmer for 5 minutes. Taste and season with 1 teaspoon of salt and ½ teaspoon of black pepper, or more if you think it needs it.

Finely chop the coriander or herb of choice, including the stalks. Divide the stew between four bowls, and sprinkle the chopped herbs over the top.

CABBAGE

Kale Pesto Pasta

This simple and delicious recipe works great with kale and also with any green leafy cabbage, such as York, Savoy or cavolo nero.

9 INGREDIENTS

1. 350g kale or green leafy cabbage

2. 140g frozen peas

3. 120g roasted red pepper, from a jar

4. 4 vegan sausages

5. 300g dried pasta of choice

6. 100g cashew nuts

7. 1 large or 2 small cloves of garlic

8. juice of 1 lime

9. a sprinkle of chilli flakes, to serve (optional)

Remove the tough centre stalks of the kale or cabbage and roughly chop the leaves. Put the frozen peas into a bowl, cover with boiling water and leave for 5 minutes to thaw. Chop the roasted red peppers and the sausages into bite-size pieces.

Put about 8–10cm of boiling water into a medium pan and add a pinch of salt. Add the chopped kale, cover with a lid and boil until steam starts to form. Steam until the leaves are tender and slightly wilted – about 3–5 minutes, depending on the type of kale/cabbage. Drain the kale, thenset aside.

Bring a large pan of salted water to the boil and add the pasta. Cook as per the instructions on the back of the packet, then take off the heat and drain, keeping a little of the starchy pasta water. Rinse the pasta and put it back into the pan.

Dry the pan you used to cook the kale and add the cashew nuts. Cook them on a medium heat for about 5–7 minutes, stirring occasionally until they start to turn golden and their delicious smell begins to fill your kitchen! Remove and set aside.

To make the pesto, peel the garlic and put it into a food processor with the toasted cashew nuts, 50g of the steamed kale or cabbage, 150ml of sunflower oil, ¾ teaspoon of salt and the lime juice, and blend until smooth. Taste and season with more salt or lemon juice if you think it needs it.

Cook the vegan sausages in a pan with 1 tablespoon of oil on a high heat for 4 minutes, turning occasionally. Drain and rinse the peas and add them to the pan with the rest of the steamed kale or cabbage and the red peppers. Cook for 3–4 minutes, stirring regularly.

Put the pan of pasta back on the heat, then add the pesto and the sausage mixture to it and mix through. If you want to make your sauce looser, just add a few tablespoons of the pasta cooking water. When everything is warmed through, serve, topped with some chilli flakes if you like a bit of spice.

CABBAGE

Middle Eastern-style Cabbage Salad

It might seem strange to have cabbage in a salad, but the strong flavours of lemon, mint and tomato really elevate it and show its surprising versatility. We make a lovely tahini dressing, which adds a richness and decadence to this salad, and serve it with some toasted bread to give it a fattoush-style feel.

9 INGREDIENTS

1. 1 medium red onion
2. 500g white cabbage
3. 1 tbsp cumin seeds
4. juice of 2 lemons
5. 80g baguette, or bread of choice
6. 25g light tahini
7. 30g fresh mint
8. 150g cherry tomatoes, ideally different colours
9. 1 fresh pomegranate

Preheat the oven to 180°C fan/200°C/gas 6.

Peel the red onion and slice into long strips. Chop the cabbage into long thin strips.

Heat 2 tablespoons of olive oil in a large saucepan on a high heat. Once hot, add the sliced onion and cumin seeds and cook for 4–5 minutes, until starting to brown slightly around the edges. Add the cabbage and ½ teaspoon of salt and fry for 8–10 minutes, stirring regularly.

Remove from the heat. Add the juice of 1½ lemons, then taste and season to your liking.

Chop the bread into 2cm cubes. Put them on a baking tray and toss with 1 tablespoon of oil. Bake for 8 minutes, then remove from the oven and set aside.

Put the tahini into a bowl along with the juice of ½ a lemon, 3 tablespoons of oil, a pinch of salt and 4 tablespoons of water, and mix well until nicely combined.

Remove the mint leaves from the stalks and finely chop. Quarter the cherry tomatoes.

Cut the pomegranate in half (sit the pomegranate crown side up and cut horizontally in half). Hold one half over a large bowl with the skin side facing up, then, using a large wooden spoon, bash the skin of the pomegranate until all the seeds are removed. Repeat with the other half of the pomegranate. Carefully remove any white skin from the seeds.

Add the chopped cherry tomatoes and mint to the cabbage and onion mixture and mix well. Taste and add more salt and ground black pepper to taste.

Drizzle the dressing over the salad just before serving, and sprinkle with the pomegranate seeds to add a beautiful brightness and bite. Lastly layer in the toasted bread and enjoy!

Teriyaki-style Tofu, Kale and Sesame Couscous

This is a take on one of our go-to dinners. It can be made in 20 minutes and always tastes so nourishing. The combination of ginger, sesame and tamari with a little splash of maple syrup is beautiful.

9 INGREDIENTS

1. 100g curly kale or cavolo nero
2. 200g firm tofu
3. 12g ginger
4. 1 red chilli
5. 100g dried wholemeal couscous
6. 3 tbsp tamari or soy sauce
7. 1 tsp apple cider vinegar or vinegar of choice
8. 1 tbsp maple syrup
9. 2 tbsp sesame seeds

Remove any firm thick stalks from the kale and rip the leaves into bite-size pieces. Slice the tofu into even-sized rectangles approx. ½cm thick. Peel the ginger and slice into very skinny strips. Finely slice the red chilli, removing the seeds if you prefer it less spicy.

Put the couscous into a bowl and add a pinch of salt and black pepper, and 1 teaspoon of olive oil. Mix well, then level the top and pour over boiling water to cover the couscous by 1cm. Cover with a large plate and leave for 5 minutes.

Pour 6cm of boiling water into a pan and add a generous pinch of salt. Add the kale, and put the pan on a high heat. Cover with a lid and bring to the boil, then reduce the heat to a simmer and leave to cook for 4 minutes. Remove from the heat and drain.

In a mug, mix together the tamari or soy sauce, vinegar and maple syrup.

Heat a non-stick pan on a high heat, and once hot, add 1 tablespoon of oil and the tofu rectangles. Press down on the tofu to evaporate any extra moisture. Allow to cook for 2–3 minutes on each side, until the tofu starts to turn golden brown.

Add the sliced ginger and stir and cook for 1 minute. Turn the heat off and add the tamari maple sauce. Be careful – there will be a nice big sizzle. As the sauce starts to reduce, turn the tofu, ensuring that there is a good glaze on each side. Remove the tofu from the pan and set aside.

Add 2 tablespoons of water and the kale to the pan. Allow to cook for 1–2 minutes, to help deglaze the pan and add more flavour to the kale. Taste and add a pinch of salt, if needed.

Use a fork to soften the couscous and remove any clumps. Divide between two plates, add the kale and tofu, and garnish with a generous sprinkling of sesame seeds and the sliced chilli.

CABBAGE

Miso-glazed Cabbage

This is one of our favourite ways to eat cabbage. It's delicious, and is always devoured in Steve's home by all the family. The charring elevates the brassica notes, and the sweet miso takes it to a whole other dimension. It makes a lovely starter or side dish.

8 INGREDIENTS

1. 1 green or York cabbage
2. 2 cloves of garlic
3. 10g ginger
4. 1 red chilli
5. 2 tbsp sesame seeds
6. 1 tbsp miso paste
7. 1 tbsp tamari or soy sauce
8. 2 tbsp maple syrup

Cut the cabbage lengthways into quarters. Peel and finely chop the garlic and ginger. Finely dice the chilli, removing the seeds, if you prefer less spice.

Put the sesame seeds into a frying pan on a medium heat and leave them to dry-fry until they start to pop. Add a pinch of salt, turn the heat off and move them around so that they brown evenly – this should take about 5 minutes. Remove them from the pan and set aside.

Heat a separate large-bottomed non-stick frying pan (with a lid) on a high heat and add 2 tablespoons of olive oil. Add the 4 quarters of the cabbage and sprinkle over ½ teaspoon of salt. Cook the cabbage on each of the two cut sides for 3–4 minutes, until it starts to char and brown. Then turn each quarter on to its back, add 2 tablespoons of water to the pan, put the lid on the pan and allow the cabbage to steam for 4 minutes.

Put the garlic, ginger, miso, tamari and maple syrup into a mug with 4 tablespoons of water and mix well. Add half this dressing to the cabbage and turn the quarters in the pan so the glaze coats both sides. Cook on each side for a further 1 minute.

Remove from the pan, and serve with the rest of the glaze drizzled over. Decorate with the diced red chilli and the toasted sesame seeds.

Cabbage and Ricotta Stuffed Pasta Shells

These giant pasta shells make a beautiful vessel for a deliciously easy cabbage and ricotta filling. We finish this dish by baking it in the oven, to melt the vegan cheese and allow the flavours to come together.

10 INGREDIENTS

1. 200g cabbage or kale
2. 2 cloves of garlic
3. 1 red chilli
4. 50g vegan Cheddar cheese
5. 150g giant pasta shells (e.g. conchiglioni)
6. 200g cashew nuts
7. 2 tsp garlic powder
8. zest and juice of ½ a lemon
9. 1 x 680g jar of tomato passata
10. 1 tbsp maple syrup

Heat the oven to 180°C fan/200°C/gas 6.

Remove and discard the cabbage or kale stalks, and finely slice the leaves. Peel and finely chop the garlic, and finely chop the red chilli. Grate the vegan Cheddar.

Cook the pasta shells following the instructions on the packet, and drain when they are still a little al dente, as they will continue to cook in the oven.

To make the cashew ricotta, half fill a small pan with boiling water and put it on a high heat, then add the cashew nuts and boil for 10 minutes. Drain and rinse the nuts well, then put them into a blender with 1 teaspoon of garlic powder, 150ml of water, the lemon zest and juice and a pinch of salt. Blend until really smooth.

Heat 1 tablespoon of oil in a wide-bottomed pan on a high heat. Once hot, add the kale or cabbage and a pinch of salt and cook for 5 minutes, stirring occasionally. Add the diced garlic and half of the chilli and cook for 1–2 minutes, then turn off the heat, add the cashew ricotta, and mix well.

To make the tomato sauce, put the tomato passata into a bowl and add 1 teaspoon of salt, 1 tablespoon of maple syrup, 1 teaspoon of garlic powder and the rest of the red chilli. Mix well and season to your liking.

Spoon the tomato sauce into the bottom of a deep lasagne-style oven dish (25 x 20cm). Using a teaspoon, fill each pasta shell with the cabbage ricotta mixture, packing it in well, then place in the dish. Dot any extra mixture over the top. Sprinkle over the grated cheese and bake in the oven for 20 minutes, until bubbling and golden.

Serve with a green salad and some garlic bread.

CABBAGE

Squash, Greens and Pesto Lasagne

Delicious, packed with flavour and full of veg, this lasagne will leave you looking for a second slice! Enjoy with a green salad and some garlic bread for a delicious centrepiece dinner. Our top tip for cutting lasagne is to use scissors.

10 INGREDIENTS

1. 200g kale or green leafy cabbage

2. 2 leeks

3. 500g butternut squash

4. 100g vegan Cheddar cheese

5. 2 x 400g tins of chopped tomatoes

6. 180g vegan pesto of choice (page 273)

7. 7 tbsp white flour

8. 750ml oat milk or plant milk of choice

9. 250g lasagne sheets

10. 30g fresh breadcrumbs

Preheat the oven to 180°C fan/200°C/gas 6.

Remove the leaves from the kale or cabbage stalks and roughly chop them. Finely chop the stalks. Slice the leeks into 1cm rounds, including the green parts, and give them a good wash. Peel the squash, remove any seeds and cut into ½cm dice. Grate all the vegan Cheddar.

Heat 1 tablespoon of oil in a large wide-bottomed non-stick pan with a lid on a high heat. Once hot, add the leeks and butternut squash along with 1 teaspoon of salt and cook for about 5 minutes, stirring regularly. Turn the heat down to medium, add the cabbage leaves and stalks, then put a lid on the pan and allow the veg to steam in their own juices for about 5 minutes, stirring occasionally. You want the leeks to be soft and the squash to be tender. Add the chopped tomatoes and the pesto. Mix well and cook for a further 5 minutes without the lid on. Season with salt and black pepper, then set aside.

To make the béchamel sauce, put 7 tablespoons of olive oil into a pan on a medium heat. Once hot, sieve in the flour and cook for 1–2 minutes, stirring continuously with a whisk until it goes slightly golden. Slowly add the oat milk, stirring continuously. Bring to the boil, then reduce to a gentle simmer, stirring to be careful that nothing sticks to the bottom. Once simmering, and when it reaches a creamy texture, remove from the heat. Add 1½ teaspoons of salt, ¾ teaspoon of ground black pepper, and mix in 25g of the vegan Cheddar. Taste and adjust the seasoning if it needs it.

To assemble the lasagne, put half the béchamel into a deep ovenproof dish (approx. 30 x 22cm), and spread it out evenly. Put a layer of lasagne sheets on top of the béchamel, ensuring that they form a single even layer at the bottom of the dish. Next, add half the tomato and veg sauce and put a single layer of lasagne sheets on top of that. Add the remaining tomato and veg sauce and top with lasagne sheets. Put the rest of the béchamel on top so that the pasta is well covered.

For the topping, mix the rest of the grated Cheddar with the breadcrumbs and 1 tablespoon of oil and sprinkle over the top. Bake in the oven for 25 minutes, until the pasta is cooked. To test, simply insert a knife or skewer and it should pass easily through the pasta. If it's not ready, just turn the heat down to avoid the top browning too much, and leave to cook for a bit longer.

Irish Stew with Colcannon Mash

This is like a warm belly hug on a cold winter's night, and defo one to try on St Patrick's Day. It's easy to make, substantial, and together with the colcannon mashed potato it is so-o-o easy to eat! You can use York or Savoy cabbage instead of kale – just steam the cabbage leaves over the boiling potatoes for a couple of minutes.

10 INGREDIENTS

1. 3 cloves of garlic
2. 2 carrots
3. 1 parsnip
4. 2 leeks
5. 1kg potatoes
6. 2 x 400g tins of cooked lentils
7. 3 tbsp tamari or soy sauce
8. 1 litre veg stock
9. 150g kale or York/Savoy cabbage
10. 150ml oat milk

To make the stew, peel and finely chop the garlic. Finely chop the carrots and the parsnip, and chop the leeks into nice 1cm chunks, making sure to include the green parts and to give them a good wash. Chop the potatoes for the mash into bite-size pieces, leaving the skins on. Set aside one chopped potato of about 200g for the stew. Drain and rinse the lentils.

Heat 1 tablespoon of oil in a large non-stick pan on a high heat. Add the chopped leeks and cook for 4 minutes, stirring occasionally. Add the carrots, parsnips, the reserved chopped potato and 1 teaspoon of salt, put the lid on the pan, then turn the heat down to medium and cook for a further 5 minutes, stirring regularly.

Add the garlic and cook for a further 1–2 minutes with no lid. Add the tamari, veg stock, lentils and ½ teaspoon of black pepper, then turn the heat back up to high and bring to the boil. Reduce to a simmer for about 15 minutes, or until the potatoes, carrots and parsnip are tender.

While the stew is simmering, put the potatoes for the mash into a large pan, cover with water and boil until soft, approx. 15–20 minutes.

Using a knife, chop the kale or cabbage, removing the tough centre ribs and finely slicing the leaves. Leave a handful aside to put through the stew before serving, to add colour.

To finish the stew, add a good pinch of black pepper, then taste and add more salt and pepper if it needs it. Finally, stir in the kale or cabbage that you put aside.

Once the potatoes are cooked, drain them and return them to the pan. Remove the pan from the heat and add the rest of the chopped kale or cabbage. Add three-quarters of the oat milk and mash it all altogether. If it seems too dry, add a little more milk – you're looking for a creamy, smooth, mashed-potato texture that is not too dry or too wet. Season with salt and black pepper (we use 1 teaspoon of salt and ½ teaspoon of pepper).

Serve the colcannon mash generously, then make a well in the centre and pour in the Irish stew for a super-comforting hearty meal.

CABBAGE

Red Ricotta and Kale Pasta Bake

A great family dinner that will go down a treat. Red ricotta sounds crazy, but we simply blend roasted red peppers through a cashew-based 'ricotta' for a beautiful colour. It also freezes really well, so this is good for batch cooking.

9 INGREDIENTS

1. 100g roasted red peppers, from a jar
2. 350g cashew nuts
3. 2½ tsp garlic powder
4. juice of 1 lemon
5. 300g kale
6. 500g cherry tomatoes
7. 125g vegan Cheddar cheese
8. 400g penne pasta (use wholemeal for a healthier option)
9. 25g fresh breadcrumbs

Preheat the oven to 180°C fan/200°C/gas 6.

Drain the roasted red peppers. Put the cashew nuts into a pan and cover with boiling water, bring back to the boil, then reduce to a simmer and cook for 10 minutes. Drain and rinse the cashews, then put into a blender with the roasted red peppers, garlic powder, lemon juice, 1 teaspoon of salt, ½ teaspoon of black pepper and 225ml of water. Blend until super-smooth.

Remove the thick stalks from the kale and finely chop the leaves. Cut the cherry tomatoes in half. Grate the vegan Cheddar.

Bring a large saucepan of water to the boil and add a pinch of salt. Add the kale and boil for 2 minutes, until just tender. Drain well, then leave in the colander and use your hands to gently press out any excess liquid. Tip the kale on to kitchen paper or a clean tea towel and give it a good squeeze to remove any remaining moisture. Add the kale to the cashew 'ricotta' and mix well.

Bring a medium pan of water to the boil and add the pasta and a tablespoon of salt. Cook as per the packet instructions, then drain and rinse with cold water to remove any starch so it doesn't stick together.

Put the drained pasta into a casserole dish about 32 x 22cm, then add the cherry tomatoes, cashew ricotta, 1 teaspoon of salt, 1 teaspoon of black pepper and 2 tablespoons of olive oil, and mix well.

Mix the breadcrumbs with the grated vegan Cheddar and 1 tablespoon of oil. Sprinkle over the top, and bake in the oven for 15 minutes.

CABBAGE

№. 5

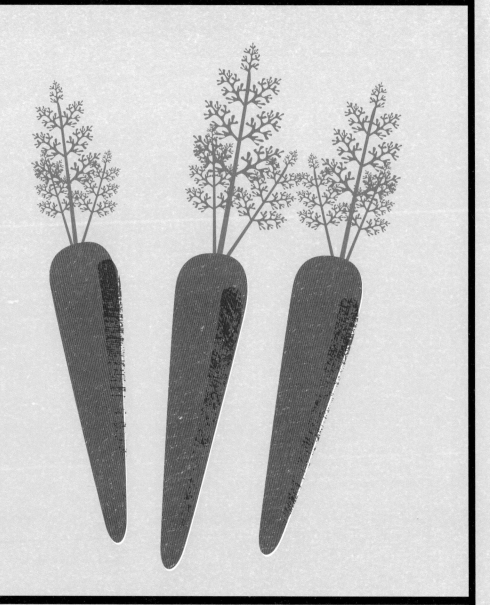

CARROTS

Carrots are one of the most versatile veg around, with their sweet flavour, bright vibrant colour and crunchy texture – and the leaves can also be used sparingly in salads.

Next to potatoes, carrots are the best known and most popular root veg of all. You can grate, slice or shave them into salads, as we show in the carrot, avocado and toasted pumpkin seed salad (page 142), eat them as a raw snack with hummus, or use them as a base for hummus, as in the carrot hummus with easy falafel nuggets (page 148), and enjoy them roasted, as we do in the Moroccan roasted carrot tagine (page 152).

Carrots were originally white or purple and native to modern-day Afghanistan or Iran. They were believed to be bitter and woody, and it wasn't until a mutation occurred that removed the purple pigmentation, resulting in a new race of yellow carrots, from which the modern-day orange carrots were developed, that people started to eat them more widely. Originally they were eaten as a herb or as a medicine, along with their seeds. It is believed that it wasn't until the seventeenth century that carrots were bred to be orange, as a tribute to the Dutch national colour and the House of Orange.

When we were growing up, carrots were limp veg served along with potatoes and the roast, and we never liked them much. It was only when we started to get into health that we realized that there was so much more to this ubiquitous root veg. As we started to cook in the café kitchen, carrots were one of the foundation veg in so many dishes: we would use them as a base for soups, grate them into salads and roast them to add to stews and curries, as well as using them to make lots of different juices in our juice bar – at times we would go through 60–100kg of carrots a day.

BUYING & STORING

Try not to peel your carrots, as a lot of the nutrients are in the skin or just beneath it. Most commercial carrots have been washed before you buy them, so just give them a good scrub before eating.

Carrots have a thin skin that can easily absorb chemicals underground. If you eat them regularly, we'd recommend you choose organic carrots, as the difference in cost can be minimal and we find the taste to be noticeably better. Carrots are best stored in the fridge in an airtight container or in the plastic bag you may have bought them in. Carrots are vascular, so if you find them starting to go limp and flaccid, put them into a tub of cold water for an hour or two and they should firm up and become more vital. Ideally, choose fresh carrots and try to support farmers and reduce food waste by choosing wonky carrots or ones that are perfectly imperfect – just like us!

GROWING

In the northern hemisphere carrots are in season from around May until September. The season usually starts with the thin, long, sweet Spanish or Italian carrots in April/May, and the Irish and UK season kicks off a month or so later.

Carrots are pretty easy to grow and they do best in loose, sandy soil. They are sown during early spring and can tolerate light frost. They usually take 2–4 months to mature. This year Steve's son Theo grew some carrots with much delight in the garden at home – they were super-easy to grow from seed. It was great to see – he started them in school with his class and he would wake up each morning to an update on the carrot seeds: 'Dad, their leaves are starting to break through the soil!' After a few weeks, in early spring, we planted them out. By mid-summer Theo was chuffed to pick his first carrot and we all shared and really savoured it!

COOKING

Carrots are the second sweetest of all veg, falling only behind beetroot. They are wonderfully accessible, widely available and, like a good Swiss army knife, are multifunctional. They are a hard root veg, so they do require a little longer when roasting compared to peppers or courgettes. Traditionally in French cooking they are part of the flavour base for soups, stocks and stews, along with onions and celery – this is called a 'mirepoix', and Italian cooking has a similar base called a 'soffritto'. In both cases the veg are generally diced finely and cooked at a low heat to develop sweetness. In this chapter we have concentrated on quicker-cooking recipes that are some of our favourites. We 'sweat' carrots, along with onions, ginger and garlic, in the warming carrot and red lentil stew (page 147), to help them release their natural sweetness. We grate and bake amazing flapjacks with them in the chewy flapjacks with carrot and pistachio (page 155), and we roast them to add sweetness and starch to the carrot and sesame burgers on page 151, along with lots of other delicious recipes to whet your carrot appetite.

NUTRITION

Just like sweet potato and pumpkin, carrots are high in beta-carotene, as evidenced by their bright orange colour. Our body converts beta-carotene into vitamin A, which is great for skin health, eyesight and immune function. The old tale our mother told us of carrots helping us to see in the dark has some good evidence – however, most people's vision is unlikely to get better from eating carrots unless they have a vitamin A deficiency. Carrots are also associated with improved digestion, cardiovascular system function and bone health. They are about 90% water and 10% carbs, crunchy and high in fibre.

CARROTS

Carrot and Maple Granola with Coconut

The carrots bring a delicious, naturally sweet carrot-cake flavour to this granola. You get to say you've had veg for breakfast, and you've already had one of your 5-a-day before leaving the house! This goes great on top of porridge or on its own with your non-dairy milk or yoghurt of choice.

9 INGREDIENTS

1. 200g carrots
2. 50g cashew nuts, or other nuts of choice
3. 50g dried apricots
4. 50g pumpkin seeds
5. 50g ground almonds
6. 50g desiccated coconut
7. 400g jumbo oat flakes
8. 120ml maple syrup
9. 25g goji berries

Preheat the oven to 160°C fan/180°C/gas 4. Line two large baking trays with baking parchment.

Peel and finely grate the carrots. Roughly chop the nuts and dried apricots. Mix a small pinch of salt with the grated carrots and place in a sieve over a bowl. Leave to sit while you prepare the other ingredients.

Put the cashew nuts into a large bowl and add the pumpkin seeds, ground almonds, desiccated coconut and oats. Mix well.

Squeeze the grated carrots to remove the excess juice (otherwise they will make your granola soggy) and put them into a bowl with the maple syrup and 100ml of vegetable oil. Mix well together.

Combine the two bowls of ingredients and mix well.

Spread the granola on the lined trays and bake for 35–40 minutes, until golden brown. Remember to stir twice during this time, to ensure that the granola bakes evenly. You can leave it longer in the oven, if you prefer more of a crunch, but take it out before it starts to burn.

Remove from the oven and leave to cool for 20 minutes. Add the chopped apricots and goji berries and mix well.

Stored in an airtight container it will easily keep for 4 weeks.

CARROTS

141

Carrot, Avocado and Toasted Pumpkin Seed Salad

This simple and delicious vibrant salad topped with toasted seeds and avocado chunks is really tasty, and very straightforward to make for a quick lunch or a side for a barbecue when carrots are bountiful. We use radicchio to give a pop of colour, but if you can't source it, just replace it with a red pepper.

9 INGREDIENTS

1. 8 carrots (750g)
2. juice of 2 limes
3. 1 head of radicchio
4. 2 tbsp sesame seeds
5. 3 tbsp pumpkin seeds
6. 2 ripe avocados
7. 20ml apple cider vinegar
8. 1 tbsp maple syrup
9. 100g rocket

Grate the carrots and put them into a large mixing bowl. Squeeze over the juice of 1 of the limes and mix (the lime juice will prevent the carrot oxidizing and going brown).

Finely slice the radicchio, removing the tough nub at the bottom, and add to the grated carrots.

Toast the sesame seeds and pumpkin seeds in a dry pan over a medium heat for about 5 minutes, stirring occasionally until they begin to pop and the lovely roasting smell starts.

Cut the avocados in half, remove the stones, then spoon out the flesh, chop it into small chunks and add to a bowl. Squeeze over the juice of the second lime, add a pinch of salt, and mix well.

To make the dressing, whisk together 60ml of olive oil with the cider vinegar, maple syrup and 1½ teaspoons of salt, until emulsified. Then stir through the carrots and radicchio.

We like to serve this salad from a big bowl, but you can serve it as individual portions if you like. Mix the rocket through the dressed carrots and radicchio. Top with the avocado and garnish with the toasted seeds.

Maple-glazed Carrot, Walnut and Cream Cheese Tartlets

These are super-comforting, and work as a lovely light lunch or starter. If you want to have these for a main meal, you can make two larger tartlets and serve them with your favourite salad. They look like you spent hours in the kitchen preparing them, but in reality they are quick to prepare and really tasty!

9 INGREDIENTS

1. 350g carrots
2. 1 red onion
3. 3 cloves of garlic
4. 1 bunch of spring onions
5. 2 tbsp maple syrup
6. 2 tbsp balsamic vinegar
7. 1 x 320g sheet of vegan ready-rolled puff pastry
8. 200g vegan cream cheese
9. 50g walnuts

Thaw your pastry if using from frozen, then preheat the oven to 200°C fan/220°C/gas 7. Line two baking trays with baking parchment.

Scrub the carrots and cut them into batons ½–1cm in diameter and 5cm long. Peel and finely slice the red onion, garlic and spring onions.

Heat 1 tablespoon of olive oil in a non-stick frying pan on a high heat, then add the carrots, sliced red onions and a pinch of salt and fry for 3–4 minutes. Add 4 tablespoons of water, reduce to a medium heat, place a lid on top and allow to cook for 5 minutes, stirring occasionally.

Remove the lid and give it all a good stir. Add the garlic, spring onions, maple syrup and balsamic vinegar and cook for 3–4 minutes, stirring regularly. Turn off the heat.

Roll out the sheet of puff pastry on a lightly floured surface so that it is about 2cm larger on all sides, and divide it into 4 equal rectangles (approx. 18 x 12½cm). Place them on the baking trays.

Break up the vegan cream cheese with a fork to make it easier to spread. In the centre of each rectangle spread 50g of cheese, leaving about 1cm of pastry uncovered around the edge and taking care not to tear the pastry.

Next, layer a quarter of the carrot and red onion mix on to each rectangle. Roughly chop the walnuts and sprinkle over the tartlets.

Bake for 15 minutes, until the pastry is golden and puffed up – don't worry if some of the cheese leaks out while baking. Remove from the oven and enjoy!

CARROTS

Carrot and Toasted Cashew Soup

A delicious, warming and hearty soup! Roasted cashews and carrots complement each other perfectly, and the cashew nuts give a lovely creamy texture. Serve with decent bread for a delightful lunch or supper.

7 INGREDIENTS

1. 3 onions
2. 3 cloves of garlic
3. 5 large carrots (650g)
4. 2 potatoes (300g)
5. 20g fresh coriander
6. 2 litres veg stock
7. 250g cashew nuts

Peel and roughly chop the onions and garlic. Leaving them unpeeled, chop the carrots and potatoes into bite-size pieces. Roughly chop the coriander stalks, keeping the leaves for garnish later.

Heat 1 tablespoon of olive oil in a large non-stick pan on a high heat. Once hot, add the onions and cook for 3–4 minutes, stirring regularly. Add the garlic, carrots, potatoes, coriander stalks and 1 teaspoon of salt and cook for another 3–4 minutes, stirring regularly. Put a lid on the pan, then reduce the heat to medium and allow the veg to cook in their own juices for 5 minutes, stirring occasionally.

Add the veg stock and turn the heat back up to high. Bring to the boil, then reduce to a simmer for a further 5–8 minutes, or until the potatoes and carrots are cooked through.

While the soup is boiling, put a wide-bottomed pan on a medium heat. Add the cashew nuts and toast them in the dry pan for about 6–8 minutes, tossing occasionally so that both sides start to toast and the room begins to fill with a lovely aroma! Remove from the heat and put a small handful (approx. 40g) of cashews aside to use as garnish.

Remove the soup from the heat and add the cashews, 1½ teaspoons of salt and ½ teaspoon of black pepper. Using an immersion blender, blend the soup until smooth. Taste and add more salt and black pepper if it needs it.

Finely chop the coriander leaves and roughly chop the rest of the toasted cashews. Serve the soup in bowls, garnished with coriander leaves and the toasted chopped cashews.

SERVES 4   **TAKES** 40 minutes

Warming Carrot and Red Lentil Stew

This is one of our favourite dishes – heart-warming, soulful and so tasty! It makes a hearty lunch or dinner that will leave you feeling deeply nourished. Lentils and carrots are a match made in heaven. Serve with decent bread and a scattering of chilli flakes, if you like a little spice.

10 INGREDIENTS

1. 2 medium onions

2. 2–3 cloves of garlic

3. 20g fresh ginger

4. 4 large carrots (500g)

5. 4 large ripe fresh tomatoes (900g) or 2 x 400g tins of chopped tomatoes

6. 30g fresh coriander

7. 350g dried split red lentils

8. 1½ tbsp medium curry powder

9. 4 tbsp tamari or soy sauce

10. juice of ½ a lemon

Peel and finely chop the onions, garlic and ginger. Finely slice the carrots. Roughly chop the tomatoes. Finely chop the coriander stalks, keeping the leaves for garnish later.

Heat 1 tablespoon of olive oil in a large non-stick pan on a high heat. Once hot, add the onions and cook for 3–4 minutes, stirring regularly. Add the carrots, garlic, ginger, tomatoes, coriander stalks, 1 teaspoon of salt and 1 teaspoon of black pepper, then put the lid on the pan and cook for another 5–6 minutes, stirring regularly.

Add the lentils, curry powder, tamari and 1.75 litres of water. Bring to the boil, stirring so the lentils don't stick, then reduce the heat to a gentle simmer and cook for a further 25–30 minutes, stirring regularly, until the lentils are properly broken down and disappear into the sauce. They should have a melt-in-your-mouth feel to them.

Squeeze in the lemon juice and mix through. Taste and season with salt and black pepper.

Serve garnished with the coriander leaves.

CARROTS

Carrot Hummus with Easy Falafel Nuggets

We make tons of hummus every week, and have done so for years. It's vegan butter to us! The only thing better than good hummus is warm hummus. Here we make a roasted carrot hummus and serve it with beautiful falafel nuggets and toasted pittas.

10 INGREDIENTS

1. 400g carrots

2. 4 medium cloves of garlic

3. 20g fresh coriander

4. 2 x 400g tins of chickpeas

5. 2 tbsp tamari or soy sauce

6. 2 tsp ground cumin

7. juice of 1½ lemons

8. 4 tbsp gram flour

9. 3 tbsp tahini

10. 4 wholemeal pitta breads

Preheat the oven to 200°C fan/220°C/gas 7. Line two baking trays with baking parchment.

Chop the carrots into 1cm rounds. Mix them with 1 teaspoon of salt and 1 tablespoon of olive oil and combine. Pour on to one of the lined baking trays and bake in the oven for 30 minutes, until cooked through and starting to char around the edges.

To make the falafel, peel and finely chop 2 of the cloves of garlic and finely chop the coriander, stalks and all. Drain and rinse both tins of chickpeas. Put the garlic and coriander into a food processor with half the chickpeas, the tamari, ground cumin, ½ teaspoon of black pepper and the juice of ½ a lemon, and blend until it comes together. Sieve in the gram flour and mix well. Shape the mixture into 16 falafel-shaped nuggets.

Put the falafel on to the second lined baking tray and brush with 1 tablespoon of oil. Bake in the oven for 20 minutes, until they crisp up, turning them halfway through so they cook evenly. Remove the falafel and finish making your hummus before serving.

To make the hummus, put the rest of the chickpeas into the food processor with the warm roasted carrots, the remaining 2 cloves of garlic, the tahini, the rest of the lemon juice, 1 tablespoon of olive oil, 1½ teaspoons of salt, 4 tablespoons of water and ½ teaspoon of black pepper. Blend until smooth.

Toast the pitta breads and serve with the hummus and falafel, along with any crudités that you may have, such as cucumber or celery sticks.

MAKES 6   **TAKES** 1 hour 20 minutes

Carrot and Sesame Burgers

These sweet and savoury burgers work great on the barbecue or cooked in a pan. We like to serve them in a bun with slices of avocado, our favourite pesto, mayo, a slice of tomato and lettuce – yum! The sesame-seed crumb gives them a nice crunch and flavour.

10 INGREDIENTS

1.	2 tbsp ground flax seed
2.	400g carrots
3.	1 x 400g tin of chickpeas
4.	20g fresh coriander
5.	100g fresh breadcrumbs
6.	100g tahini
7.	2 tbsp tamari or soy sauce
8.	3 tbsp nutritional yeast
9.	juice of ½ a lemon
10.	6 tbsp sesame seeds

Preheat the oven to 200°C fan/220°C/gas 7. Line a baking tray with baking parchment.

Put the ground flax seed into a bowl and add 6 tablespoons of water. Stir well, then leave to stand for 3–5 minutes to form a 'flax egg' – this will help to bind the burger ingredients.

Cut the carrots into 1cm rounds. Drain and rinse the chickpeas. Finely chop the coriander, stalks and all. Place the carrots on a baking tray. Add 1 teaspoon of salt and 1 tablespoon of olive oil and mix, coating the carrots well. Bake in the oven for 30 minutes, then remove from the oven and leave to cool so that more moisture evaporates and they become sweeter.

Put the chickpeas into a food processor with the roasted carrots and pulse for a couple of minutes, then add the flax egg, breadcrumbs, tahini, tamari, nutritional yeast, lemon juice, coriander, 1 teaspoon of salt and ½ teaspoon of black pepper, and pulse again until it all comes together but still has a bit of texture.

Put the sesame seeds into a bowl. Shape the mixture into 6 burger-shaped patties and dip each one into the sesame seeds, turning so that each side gets a covering. Chill the burgers in the fridge for 10 minutes – this will firm them up and make them easier to handle when frying or barbecuing.

Fry the burgers for 3–4 minutes on each side on a hot barbecue or in a wide-bottomed non-stick pan on a medium to high heat, taking care not to burn the sesame seeds. To make them crispier, cook them in 1 tablespoon of oil or bake them in the oven at 200°C fan/220°C/ gas 7 for 20 minutes, making sure to turn them halfway through so they cook evenly.

Serve in your favourite bun with your toppings of choice.

CARROTS

Moroccan Roasted Carrot Tagine

After a busy day, let the oven do the hard work for you. A tagine gets its name from the casserole dish it is baked in. This freezes well and will keep for 3 days in the fridge. The contrasting sweet and savoury in this slow-cooked tagine really complement each other and it is a favourite with our families! We love to serve this with coconut yoghurt and finely chopped mint.

10 INGREDIENTS

1. 1 large onion

2. 3 cloves of garlic

3. 4 carrots

4. 1 x 400g tin of chopped tomatoes

5. ½ tsp ground cinnamon

6. 1 tsp smoked paprika

7. 2 tsp ground cumin

8. 1 x 400g tin of chickpeas

9. 3 tbsp raisins

10. 5 tbsp flaked almonds

Preheat the oven to 200°C/220°C/gas 7.

Peel and finely chop the onion and garlic. Grate one of the carrots. Put the onion, garlic and grated carrot into a blender along with the tinned tomatoes, cinnamon, ½ teaspoon of smoked paprika, cumin, 1 teaspoon of salt and ½ teaspoon of black pepper, and blend until smooth.

Drain and rinse the chickpeas and put them into a casserole dish along with the blended tomato sauce, the raisins, 400ml of water, 1½ teaspoons of salt and ½ teaspoon of black pepper. Bake in the oven for 25 minutes.

Meanwhile, finely slice the remaining carrots at an angle into ½cm slices. Put them on a separate baking tray, add 2 tablespoons of oil, a pinch of salt and ½ teaspoon of smoked paprika, and mix well. Bake in the oven for 25 minutes.

While the tagine and carrots are baking, heat a non-stick frying pan on a medium heat. Once hot, add the flaked almonds and fry for 5 minutes, stirring occasionally, until they are golden.

Take the tagine and carrots out of the oven, and add the roasted carrots to the tagine. Garnish with the toasted almonds, add some coconut yoghurt and chopped mint if you have any, then serve in the middle of the table and let everyone tuck in!

Chewy Flapjacks with Carrot and Pistachio

These are so good, and they are a great way to sneak some extra veg into your day. Carrots are the second sweetest of all the veg and really complement the chewy goodness of these flapjacks beautifully!

7 INGREDIENTS

1. 100g carrots

2. 200g pistachios (in the shell)

3. 200g jumbo oats

4. 75g plain flour

5. 125g brown sugar of choice

6. 150g vegetable oil

7. 50ml maple syrup

Preheat the oven to 160°C fan/180°C/gas 4. (For a crispier flapjack, bake them at 180°C fan/200°C/gas 6.) Line a 28 x 18cm brownie tray with baking parchment.

Peel and finely grate the carrots. Mix them with a tiny pinch of salt and set them in a sieve over a bowl, squeezing out any extra juice.

Shell the pistachios (you should have about 100g) and roughly chop, setting aside 2 tablespoons for garnish.

In a bowl, mix the oats, flour, brown sugar and chopped pistachios and make a well in the middle. In another bowl, mix the grated carrot, vegetable oil and maple syrup. Then add the wet ingredients to the dry ingredients and mix well.

Put the flapjack mixture into the lined tin, pressing it into the corners and flattening it gently with the back of a spoon so it is well compacted. Bake for 30 minutes.

Remove from the oven, sprinkle over the remaining chopped pistachios and gently press into the cooked flapjack so they don't fall off when cool.

While still in the tray and warm, portion into 16 squares, using a knife. Then allow to cool fully before removing from the tray.

Store in an airtight container. We don't actually know how much longer than 7 days they keep at ambient room temperature, as they are always eaten before then!

CARROTS

Easy Carrot Cake Cupcakes

These are light and creamy, and they are that perfect small delicate size that makes you feel like you're not over-indulging and you might have a second one!

9 INGREDIENTS

1. 50g walnuts, plus 12 to decorate

2. 50g raisins

3. 200g self-raising flour

4. 150g light brown muscovado sugar

5. 1 tsp ground cinnamon

6. ½ tsp ground allspice

7. 100g carrots

8. 220g vegan cream cheese

9. 75g icing sugar

Preheat the oven to 180°C fan/200°C/gas 6. Line a standard 12-muffin tray with cupcake liners.

Roughly chop the 50g of walnuts. Put them into a large bowl with the raisins, flour, brown sugar, cinnamon, allspice and a small pinch of salt, and mix well.

Peel and grate the carrots and put them into a second bowl with 140ml of vegetable oil and 90ml of water. Mix well.

Add the wet ingredients to the dry ingredients and mix well again. Divide the mixture evenly between the cupcake cases. Bake for 20 minutes until a skewer comes out clean.

Make the icing while the cakes are in the oven. Put the vegan cream cheese into a bowl and mash with a fork, so it will be easier to mix with the icing sugar. Sift in the icing sugar, using a sieve so there are no lumps. Using a whisk or a fork, whisk the vegan cream cheese and icing sugar until smooth. Pop the icing into the fridge until ready to use.

Take the cupcakes out of the oven and leave to cool. Once fully cool, ice them with either a piping bag or a spoon. Pop a walnut on top of each cupcake.

NO. 6

CAULIFLOWER

We used to hate cauliflower and never used it. It didn't feature at all in our first couple of cookbooks, as we had it labelled as bland and unworthy of our attention.

We reckon this was because when we were growing up our only exposure to cauliflower was cauliflower cheese, and we dreaded it when that was for dinner. It wasn't until a friend baked cauliflower for us one evening that we did a 180-degree turn on it and our love affair with cauliflower began. Like courgettes, at first glance they can come across a little watery, but once roasted and some of that moisture evaporates, their true magnificence shines through.

Cauliflower is part of the brassica family, related to broccoli and cabbage. It is a variety of cabbage in which the flowers have begun to bud (the white part) but have stopped growing. In fact, if you leave cauliflowers to their own devices and don't harvest them, they will revert back to being wild cabbages after about ten seasons.

Cauliflower comes with purple and yellow and green florets, as well as the more commonly known white. The cauliflower that wins the prize for the weirdest and also the most amazing-looking of all veg is romanesco. We think that if aliens landed and planted their own veg this is what they would look like!

BUYING & STORING

Look for cauliflowers with leaves that curl around the florets. If a cauliflower is really fresh, the leaves will look vibrant and bright green. Don't be put off by any little rust spots on the florets, and there is no need to look for a whiter-than-white head – yellow is fine, but white turning to yellow is not.

Keep the leaves on when storing your cauliflower, as once you start to peel them back it will brown quicker. Store it in the fridge for 3–5 days.

GROWING

Cauliflower is really suited to growing in the UK and Irish climate – it loves our damp maritime conditions and can be harvested eleven out of the twelve months a year in coastal areas. Therefore it is by and large seldom unavailable in Ireland and the UK, with different varieties planted throughout the warmer months to ensure a year-round supply.

There are two categories of cauliflower – summer and winter – so it is either planted in early spring and harvested in June to October, or else planted in autumn for a November to May harvest. Summer cauliflowers are really quick to grow, and in as little as fifty days you can be eating your own home-grown cauliflower. In winter it is slow-growing and can take a full year to grow. Most of the winter caulis are grown in coastal areas where the frost isn't severe, and many tend to be imported from France and Holland.

COOKING

Baking florets in the oven with a little oil and salt reveals cauliflower's succulent deliciousness (often we parboil it to speed up this process). By roasting cauliflower it transforms what you may think as a plain crunchy veg into a dish worthy of your favourite guests. Cauliflower can be steamed, boiled, fried and even turned into steaks.

We roast some cauliflower 'steaks' to go on top of our cauliflower curry bake on page 170. We use it to make soup, rice or pizza bases, such as the cauliflower pizza base with pesto Parmesan topping (page 175). Steve even has a recipe for a stuffed roasted cauliflower Wellington (page 179). And it's great with spices, on its own or in a curry like the cauliflower and potato curry (page 173).

The leaves are also delicious baked in the oven – just chop the large ones in half lengthways so they cook in a similar time to the florets. It is a seriously versatile veg, and one we are huge believers in!

NUTRITION

Cauliflower is high in vitamin C and is a good source of folic acid, which helps our body produce and maintain new cells. It is high in fibre and water and, like most veg, low in calories. Its soluble fibre means that it helps our digestive system, and it also contains the antioxidant sulforaphane, which really helps boost our immune system.

The average cauliflower weighs approximately 580g, so about ⅐ of a head of cauliflower or 80g of cauliflower is considered one of your 5-a-day.

Buffalo Cauliflower Wings

This recipe is used on the bar snack menu of a local 5-star hotel, where we've designed the vegan menu. They are delicious on their own, dunked in your favourite sauce, or alternatively we love to serve them with a simple mashed avocado, a squeeze of lime, vegan mayo and pickled red onion in tacos – they are so-o-o tasty!

10 INGREDIENTS

1. 1 head of cauliflower

2. 100g plain white flour

3. 3 tsp paprika

4. 4 tsp garlic powder

5. 180ml oat milk or non-dairy milk of choice

6. 2 tbsp tomato purée

7. 2 tbsp apple cider vinegar

8. 2 tbsp maple syrup

9. 1 tsp chilli powder (or ½ tsp if you are sensitive to spice)

10. vegan mayo (page 275), to serve

Preheat the oven to 200°C fan/220°C/gas 7. Line a baking tray with baking parchment.

Cut the cauliflower into bite-size florets, removing the tough stalk.

Put the flour into a large mixing bowl with 1 teaspoon of paprika, 1 teaspoon of garlic powder, 1 teaspoon of salt and ½ teaspoon of black pepper, and mix well. Add the oat milk and mix well. Add the cauliflower florets and coat them evenly in the sauce.

Transfer the coated cauliflower to the baking tray and roast in the oven for 20 minutes, until starting to char.

Meanwhile make the buffalo hot sauce. Put 4 tablespoons of olive oil and 2 tablespoons of water into a bowl with 1 teaspoon of salt, 2 teaspoons of paprika, 3 teaspoons of garlic powder, the tomato purée, vinegar, maple syrup and chilli powder, and whisk together until smooth.

Remove the cauliflower from the oven. Using a pastry brush, cover each of the cauliflower florets with the hot sauce, making sure you give each side a good coating. Put back into the oven and bake for a further 20 minutes.

Remove from the oven and allow to cool for a couple of minutes. Serve with vegan mayo.

Peanut Tofu and Greens with Cauliflower Rice

A tasty, straightforward dinner that transforms cauliflower into rice, which we top with super-flavoursome tofu cubes and chilli greens. This dish is high in fibre, along with protein-rich tofu, and has a nice variety of texture and tastes.

10 INGREDIENTS

1. 300g tofu

2. 100g spring onions

3. 1 large head of bok choy

4. ½ a red chilli

5. 2 cloves of garlic

6. 1 medium head of cauliflower

7. 3 tbsp smooth peanut butter or almond butter

8. 1 tbsp maple syrup

9. 5 tbsp tamari or soy sauce

10. ½ tsp chilli powder

Drain the block of tofu and chop into small bite-size cubes. Chop the spring onions into small bite-size pieces. Chop off the nub at the end of the bok choy and slice the leaves lengthways into long strips. Finely chop the red chilli, removing the seeds if you don't like too much spice. Peel and finely chop the garlic.

Grate the cauliflower, using a box grater or the grater attachment on a food processor. Finely chop the stalk of the cauliflower and remove the centre stalk of the cauliflower leaves. You should get approx. 500g of cauliflower.

Heat 1 tablespoon of olive oil in a large non-stick pan on a high heat. Add the tofu and cook for 5 minutes, stirring occasionally until it starts to turn golden all over.

While the tofu is cooking, put the peanut butter into a small bowl with the maple syrup, 3 tablespoons of tamari, chilli powder and 3 tablespoons of oil and mix together until smooth.

Add the sauce to the tofu and stir until it is absorbed and the tofu is coated evenly. Remove the tofu from the pan and set aside.

Put a second pan on a medium heat. Add the grated cauliflower, chopped cauliflower stalk and leaves along with 1 tablespoon of tamari and cook for about 5 minutes. Add the chopped garlic and cook for a further 2 minutes, stirring occasionally, until it starts to brown slightly and become tender. Remove the pan from the heat and keep covered with a lid to keep warm.

Heat 1 tablespoon of oil on a high heat in the pan you used for the tofu. Once hot, add the bok choy, spring onions and chilli and cook for 2–3 minutes, stirring regularly. Drizzle 1 tablespoon of tamari over the greens and chilli. Add the tofu to the pan and heat through for 2 minutes. Fill your bowls with the cauliflower rice and the tofu and garnish with the chilli greens.

We like to serve this with a little crimson or red cabbage sauerkraut for a pop of colour and some gut-friendly bacteria!

CAULIFLOWER

SERVES 4   **TAKES** 40 minutes

Rainbow Roasted Cauliflower Salad

Yellow roasted cauliflower with succulent sweet leeks and aubergines on a bed of couscous, topped with a sweet tahini orange dressing and some ruby-like pomegranate seeds – this is a regal salad that is every bit as tasty as it is visually stimulating! Enjoy it warm or cold, and only dress as much as you are going to eat at a time.

10 INGREDIENTS

1. 1 head of cauliflower
2. 2 tsp ground turmeric
3. 1 medium aubergine
4. 2 leeks
5. 100g frozen peas
6. 100g wholemeal couscous
7. juice of 2 small oranges
8. 4 tbsp light tahini
9. 1½ tbsp maple syrup
10. 1 pomegranate

Preheat the oven to 200°C fan/220°C/gas 7.

Cut the cauliflower head into florets, removing the tough centre stalk. Put the florets into a mixing bowl.

Put the turmeric, 4 tablespoons of olive oil, 8 tablespoons of water, 1½ teaspoons of salt and ½ teaspoon of black pepper into a cup and mix well. Add to the cauliflower, making sure each piece is coated well. If you want really yellow cauliflower, put on some kitchen gloves and massage in the dressing. Spread the coated cauliflower on a baking tray and bake in the oven for 25 minutes.

Meanwhile, chop the aubergine into bite-size pieces and put them into a clean mixing bowl. Add 2 tablespoons of oil and a pinch of salt, and mix well, so that each piece is well coated. Spread the aubergine on a baking tray and bake in the oven for 25 minutes.

Slice the leeks into 3cm chunks, including the green parts, and give them a good wash. Heat a frying pan on a high heat and, once hot, add 1 tablespoon of oil. Add the chopped leeks and cook, stirring once or twice, until they start to char – this should take approx. 3–4 minutes. Reduce the heat to medium, then add 2–3 tablespoons of water and cover with a lid so that the leeks start to steam. Continue to cook them for 10 minutes, stirring occasionally. Remove the leeks from the pan and set aside. They should be soft and succulent!

Put the frozen peas into a bowl and cover with boiling water. Leave to thaw for 10 minutes, then drain.

Put the couscous into a mixing bowl and add a pinch of salt and ground black pepper. Pour over boiling water, so that it comes 1cm above the top of the couscous. Cover with a plate and leave for 5 minutes.

To make the dressing, whisk the orange juice with the tahini, maple syrup, 3 tablespoons of oil, ½ teaspoon of salt and ¼ teaspoon of black pepper.

To remove the seeds from the pomegranate cut it in half widthways. Hold one half over a bowl and, using a wooden spoon, bash the top of the skin to remove the seeds. Repeat with the other half and remove any white pith.

Put the couscous into a large salad platter/bowl, fluffing it up with a fork. Top with the roasted veg and the peas, and drizzle the dressing over. Finally garnish with the pomegranate seeds.

Roasted Cauliflower and Hazelnut Creamy Spaghetti

Cauliflower is at its best when charred or roasted. This brings out its creamy sweetness, which contrasts against the slightly acidic, crispy, caramel flavour. The roasted cauliflower in this dish cuts through the sauce with bursts of crunchy toasted hazelnuts. This makes a wonderfully comforting dinner and a delicious lunch.

10 INGREDIENTS

1. 1 head of cauliflower
2. 1 medium red onion
3. 100g hazelnuts
4. 400g dried spaghetti
5. 1 whole head of garlic
6. 1 tbsp tamari or soy sauce
7. 1 tsp smoked paprika
8. 4 tbsp plain white flour
9. 400ml oat milk, or plant milk of choice
10. juice of ½ a lemon

Preheat the oven to 200°C fan/220°C/gas 7.

Cut the head of cauliflower into bite-size florets and chop the leaves. Peel and finely slice the red onion.

Put the hazelnuts on a baking tray and bake for 10 minutes. Remove from the oven and, once cool enough to handle, place in the centre of a clean tea towel. Bring the edges of the tea towel together so the hazelnuts are covered and roughly rub until the skins start to remove and loosen. Remove and discard the skins. Roughly chop the hazelnuts.

Cook the spaghetti in a pan of boiling water according to the packet instructions. Drain and keep warm.

Bring another pan of water to the boil and add a generous pinch of salt. Add the cauliflower florets and leaves and cook for 5 minutes. Drain and leave to steam dry in the colander for a minute or so.

Cut the top off the head of garlic, exposing the top of each clove, then wrap in a square of foil. Put the wrapped garlic on a baking tray with the cauliflower, onion, tamari, smoked paprika, 2 tablespoons of olive oil and a generous pinch of salt. Mix well and bake for 20 minutes.

To make the béchamel sauce, place a saucepan on a high heat and add 4 tablespoons of oil. Once hot, sieve in the flour and cook for 1–2 minutes, stirring continuously. Slowly add the oat milk, whisking all the time. Bring to the boil, then reduce to a simmer for 3–4 minutes, until the sauce thickens to a nice creamy consistency.

Remove the roasted garlic from the oven and squeeze the cloves out of the skin. Add these to the white sauce along with the lemon juice, and blend using an immersion or stick blender. Add ¾ teaspoon of salt and a pinch of black pepper and mix until smooth. Taste and season if it needs it.

To bring the dish together add the cooked spaghetti to the sauce along with the roasted onion, half the roasted hazelnuts and half the roasted cauliflower. Gently warm on a medium heat for 2 minutes, stirring occasionally, to bring the flavours together.

Divide between three or four plates and decorate with the rest of the roasted cauliflower and hazelnuts.

CAULIFLOWER

Cauliflower Curry Bake

This is a delicious pan bake where we simply prep the curry and sauce, put them in the oven, make some charred cauliflower 'steaks' to go on top, and that's it – dinner ready! This goes great served with rice for a filling family dinner. Use your herb of choice – fresh coriander, flat-leaf parsley or chives work well.

10 INGREDIENTS

1. 3 cloves of garlic

2. 1 x 400ml tin of coconut milk

3. 400ml veg stock

4. 1½ tbsp medium curry powder

5. 4 tbsp tamari or soy sauce

6. 500g sweet potato or butternut squash

7. 6 vegan sausages, defrosted if frozen

8. 1 medium leek

9. 1 head of cauliflower

10. 10g fresh herbs of choice

Preheat the oven to 200°C fan/220°C/gas 7.

To make the sauce, peel and roughly chop the garlic, put it into a blender with the coconut milk, stock, curry powder and 3 tablespoons of tamari, and blend until smooth.

Chop the sweet potato or butternut squash into bite-size pieces (remove the seeds and skin from the squash). Chop the sausages into bite-size pieces. Slice the leek, including the green parts, into nice bite-size rounds of approx. 1–2cm and give them a good wash. Put all the veg and sausages into a large deep oven dish (we use a 32 x 22cm dish) with the sauce and mix together.

Cut the cauliflower into four equal-sized 'steaks', chopping it from the top to the bottom, and cut the leaves into thin strips. Place the cauliflower steaks on a separate baking tray along with any smaller pieces of cauliflower that have broken off and the cauliflower leaves. Brush with 2 tablespoons of olive oil, drizzle over the remaining 1 tablespoon of tamari, and sprinkle with salt.

Put the oven dish and the baking tray of cauliflower into the oven and bake for 30–40 minutes, or until the sweet potato or squash is soft and cooked through and the cauliflower is soft and slightly charred round the edges.

Remove the dish and tray from the oven. Place the roasted cauliflower on top of the sauce and veg, garnish with the chopped fresh herbs, and enjoy!

Charred Cauliflower and Pine Nut Spaghetti

A tasty, elegant pasta dinner, with melt-in-your-mouth charred cauliflower and toasted pine nuts combined with a simple garlic and chilli-infused spaghetti, and topped with crunchy breadcrumbs. Try to use wholemeal spaghetti, as it is much higher in fibre than white spaghetti. If you like vegan Parmesan or nutritional yeast, these are nice to serve with along with some garlic bread.

9 INGREDIENTS

1. 1 medium head of cauliflower
2. 200g dried spaghetti
3. 30g pine nuts
4. 40g dried breadcrumbs
5. 2 small red onions
6. 1½ tbsp balsamic vinegar
7. 3 cloves of garlic
8. 1 red chilli
9. 100ml white wine

Preheat the oven to 220°C fan/240°C/gas 9.

Cut the cauliflower into florets, removing the stalk, and cut the cauliflower leaves into small strips. Put them into a mixing bowl and toss them with 2 tablespoons of olive oil and ½ teaspoon of salt. Put them on a baking tray in the oven for 25 minutes, to roast and char.

Cook the spaghetti in a large pan of lightly salted boiling water as per the instructions on the packet. Then drain, reserving some of the cooking water.

Toast the pine nuts and breadcrumbs in a dry pan over a medium heat for 5 minutes, until they start to turn golden, then remove from the pan and set aside.

Peel the red onions and chop into half-moons. Put them into a bowl and add the balsamic vinegar and a pinch of salt. Mix well. Peel and finely chop the garlic. Finely slice the chilli, leaving the seeds in if you like a bit of heat – discard the seeds if you want it less spicy.

Heat 1 tablespoon of oil in a wide-bottomed non-stick pan on a high heat. Once hot, add the onions and cook for 4–5 minutes, stirring regularly, until they start to go translucent. Add the garlic and chilli and cook for a further 2 minutes, stirring regularly. Add the white wine and allow to bubble angrily until two-thirds of it has reduced.

Add the cooked spaghetti to the pan and reduce the heat right down low. Add a little of the reserved pasta water to moisten the dish and mix well. Mix in the roasted cauliflower.

Serve garnished with the toasted pine nuts and breadcrumbs. If you want to make it more indulgent, add a drizzle of olive oil!

Cauliflower and Potato Curry

This is a blend of two of our favourite dishes, a Bombay potato curry and an aloo gobi, which results in a wonderful roasted cauliflower potato curry that is wholesome, tasty and very straightforward to make. It goes great served with brown rice, or even with toasted pitta breads with some mango chutney for lunch.

10 INGREDIENTS

1. 1 head of cauliflower

2. 3 tbsp curry powder

3. 1 leek

4. 850g potatoes (ideally a waxy potato like a Rooster)

5. 150g frozen peas

6. 1 tbsp mustard seeds (black seeds look better)

7. 1x 400ml tin of coconut milk

8. 1x 400g tin of chopped tomatoes

9. 2 tbsp tamari or soy sauce

10. 1 small bunch of fresh coriander

Preheat the oven to 200°C fan/220°C/gas 7.

Remove the hard tough stalk and leaves from the cauliflower. Cut the thick stems from the leaves and slice into thin strips, then cut the florets into small pieces and put them on a baking tray. Add 3 tablespoons of olive oil, 2 tablespoons of curry powder and ½ teaspoon of salt, and mix well, ensuring that you coat the cauliflower florets. Bake in the oven for 30 minutes.

Meanwhile, chop the leek into small rounds and give them a good wash. Chop the potatoes into bite-size pieces. Put the frozen peas into a bowl of boiling water and leave to sit for 10 minutes.

Heat 1 tablespoon of oil in a wide-bottomed non-stick pan on a high heat. Add the leek and cook for 4 minutes, stirring regularly. Add the potatoes, mustard seeds and 1 teaspoon of salt and cook for a further 2 minutes, stirring throughout. Add 2 tablespoons of water, then turn the heat down to medium, put a lid on the pan and leave to cook for 10–15 minutes, stirring occasionally. Check to see that the potatoes are soft and cooked through.

Remove the lid and add the coconut milk, chopped tomatoes, tamari, remaining curry powder and ½ teaspoon of black pepper. Turn the heat up high and bring to the boil. Then reduce to a simmer until the potatoes are cooked. Drain and rinse the peas.

When the roasted cauliflower is ready, add it to the dish along with the peas, keeping some cauliflower aside for the garnish. Finely chop the coriander, including the stalks.

Serve, garnished with the cauliflower you put aside and the chopped coriander.

CAULIFLOWER

Cauliflower Pizza Base with Pesto Parmesan Topping

A simple and delicious cauliflower pizza base that happens to be gluten-free. You can replace our toppings with your favourite pizza toppings of choice – one of our favourites is oyster mushrooms marinated in a little tamari. Serve this with some fresh rocket for a peppery bite, and if you like olives they give it a lovely salty hit.

10 INGREDIENTS

1. 1 head of cauliflower (700g)
2. 1 tbsp ground flax seed
3. 1 tsp garlic powder
4. 2 tbsp nutritional yeast
5. 50g vegan Cheddar cheese
6. 100g ground almonds
7. 80g gram flour
8. 100g pesto (page 273)
9. 100g tomato purée
10. 80g vegan Parmesan cheese

Preheat the oven to 180°C fan/200°C/gas 6 and boil the kettle.

Break the cauliflower florets off the main stalk and put them in a steamer or, if you don't have one, just put them in a colander over a pot of boiling water and seal with a lid to steam for 8 minutes.

Put the ground flax seed into a small bowl and add 3 tablespoons of water. Stir well and leave to sit for 5 minutes. This will make a 'flax egg'.

Drain the cauliflower into a colander and leave to sit for 2 minutes while the steam evaporates, then leave to cool for 5 minutes. Pat them with kitchen paper to dry them out.

Put the cauliflower into a food processor and blitz until it reaches a rice/couscous consistency. Transfer it to a clean tea towel, cover, and squeeze out as much water as possible by wringing it very tightly. This will give us a firmer base. It's best to do this in 2 batches. Remove to a mixing bowl.

Add the 'flax egg' to the bowl, along with the garlic powder, nutritional yeast, vegan Cheddar, ground almonds, gram flour and 1 teaspoon of salt. Mix well, incorporating everything together, then divide in half.

Line two baking trays with parchment paper and spray with a little oil so that the bases come off easily after baking. Using a spatula or clean hands, press the cauliflower pizza dough into two round, even pizza base shapes, approx. 22cm in diameter, one per baking tray. Prick the pizza bases 4 or 5 times, using a fork. Bake in the oven for 30 minutes.

Remove the pizza bases from the oven, then mix the pesto and the tomato purée together and divide it between both bases, spreading it out to the edges. Roughly chop the olives and sprinkle on top of both pizzas along with the vegan parmesan, then put it back in the oven for 15 minutes.

Remove and scatter over some rocket leaves, then slice and enjoy!

CAULIFLOWER

Roasted Harissa Cauliflower with Warm Hummus and Za'atar

This makes a wonderful sharing platter and is such a beautiful centrepiece, celebrating one of our favourite ways to eat cauliflower. Za'atar is a spice mix that we love, and we have created our own simplified version to combine perfectly with the spice of harissa paste for a real flavour explosion. We've used shop-bought harissa here, but you can also make your own (see page 272).

9 INGREDIENTS

1. 1 head of cauliflower

2. 2½ tbsp harissa sauce (page 272)

3. 50g pine nuts

4. 2 tbsp sesame seeds

5. 2 tbsp cumin seeds

6. 2 x 400g tins of chickpeas

7. 2 cloves of garlic

8. 4 tbsp tahini

9. juice of 1 lemon

Preheat the oven to 200°C fan/220°C/gas 7.

Cut the cauliflower into florets, and remove and discard the tough centre rib from the leaves. Put the florets and leaves into a mixing bowl. Add 4 tablespoons of olive oil, a good pinch of salt and 2 tablespoons of harissa and mix well, coating all the cauliflower and leaves. Transfer to a baking tray and bake for 25 minutes, removing the leaves after 15 minutes, as otherwise they'll burn.

For the za'atar, put the pine nuts, sesame seeds and cumin seeds into a dry frying pan over a medium heat and leave for about 5 minutes, stirring regularly until they start to brown and smell toasty. Be careful not to burn the pine nuts. Put them into a pestle and mortar with ½ teaspoon of salt and a good pinch of black pepper, and grind until you reach a breadcrumb texture. (If you don't have a pestle and mortar, just place everything in a ziplock bag and use a mug to bash them until they reach a breadcrumb consistency.)

For the hummus, drain and rinse the chickpeas and peel the garlic. Put a pan of boiling water on a high heat and add the chickpeas. Cook for 10 minutes, to warm them through. Drain the chickpeas and put them into a food processor with the garlic cloves, tahini, lemon juice, 1½ teaspoons of salt and a good pinch of black pepper. Add 8 tablespoons of water and blend until super-smooth.

Mix the remaining ½ tablespoon of harissa with 3 tablespoons of oil to make a harissa oil.

Spread the hummus on a serving plate and top with the roasted harissa cauliflower. Drizzle over the harissa oil and garnish with about 3 tablespoons of za'atar (put any leftover za'atar into an airtight container in the fridge, where it will keep for up to two weeks). Any leftover hummus will last for 3–5 days in an airtight container in the fridge.

SERVES 2–4   **TAKES** 1 hour 20 minutes

Stuffed Roasted Cauliflower Wellington

Think cauliflower stuffed with an Italian pesto and teriyaki sauce and all wrapped in puff pastry – this is an all-singing-all-dancing cauliflower centrepiece!

9 INGREDIENTS

1. 75g cashew nuts

2. 1 large cauliflower

3. 20g fresh basil

4. 1 clove of garlic

5. juice of ¼ of a lemon

6. 1 tbsp tamari or soy sauce

7. 1 tbsp maple syrup

8. 1 x 320g sheet of vegan ready-rolled puff pastry

9. 30ml oat milk or plant milk of choice

Preheat the oven to 180°C fan/200°C/gas 6.

Put the cashews on a baking tray and bake for 6–7 minutes in the oven until toasted. Remove from the oven and set aside, then increase the heat to 200°C fan/220°C/gas 7. Line a second baking tray with baking parchment.

Remove the leaves and base stalk from the cauliflower. Put the whole cauliflower into a large saucepan, cover it with 300ml of boiling water and add a pinch of salt, put the lid on and bring it to the boil on a high heat. Then reduce the heat and simmer for 8 minutes. Drain the cauliflower and leave it in the colander for 2 minutes to allow any excess water to run off.

Meanwhile make the pesto. Roughly chop the basil. Peel and chop the garlic. Put the toasted cashew nuts, chopped basil and garlic, lemon juice, ½ teaspoon of salt and 75ml of olive oil into a food processor and blend until really smooth. Set aside.

Mix together the tamari, maple syrup and 1 tablespoon of oil to make a marinade. Place the cauliflower in a mixing bowl and pour over the marinade, making sure any extra sauce is smeared into the centre of the cauliflower. Transfer to the lined baking tray and bake for 25 minutes until nice and golden, and charred in some places.

Once the cauliflower is cool enough to touch, roll out the puff pastry on a lightly floured surface so that it is approx. 3mm thick and big enough to cover the full cauliflower. Spoon a third of the pesto into the middle of this pastry and spread it around. Fill a piping bag (or a sealable ziplock bag with a fine cut in the corner) with the remaining pesto and start to fill in between the cauliflower florets and the base, easing them open slightly if necessary. If any of the large florets come away, not to worry – just fit them back in place after filling. Make sure the cauliflower is well stuffed with pesto.

Place the cauliflower upside down on top of the pastry and pull the ends of the pastry up and over, overlapping as you go, so the cauliflower is fully sealed in the pastry with no gaps.

Carefully turn it over so the ends of the pastry are tucked underneath, and place your cauliflower Wellington on the lined baking tray, right way up. Brush with a little oat milk and bake for 20–25 minutes until golden!

Serve with mushroom gravy (page 271), some roast potatoes and veg.

Nº. 7

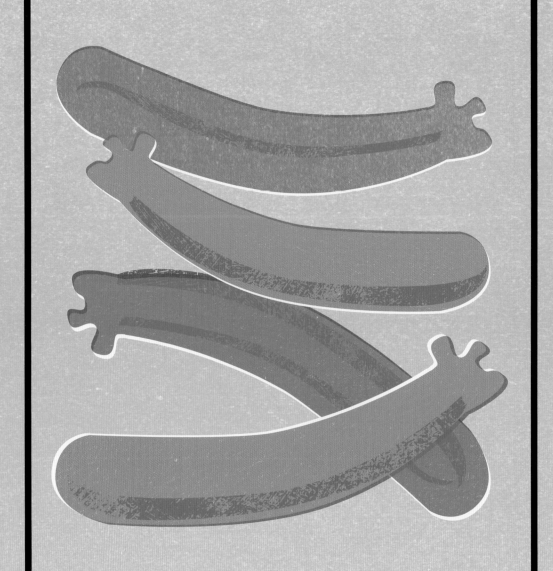

COURGETTES

The first time we really tasted courgettes and succumbed to their subtle taste was when we started grilling them on the barbecue.

Grilling courgettes with a little olive oil and salt really unlocks their secret song, a sweet, subtle tang that will have you looking for more! Courgettes are more than 90% water, so often they can take a while to char or brown and release their sweetness. Like beetroot they lend themselves to being included in desserts, as their flavour is gentle and combines beautifully with citrus fruit, so we have two desserts in this section: a courgette and lemon loaf cake with a lemon curd (page 200) and some courgette and lime cupcakes (page 199).

Courgettes are part of the cucurbit family, which is the same family as cucumber, squash and melon. Technically a courgette is a fruit, as it contains a seed, but we eat it as a veg, when it is young and the skin hasn't become hard and tough like a full-grown marrow. A marrow is an overgrown courgette – they can sometimes reach a weight of up to 5kg! One of our first encounters with a marrow was with this gentleman called George who used to come into the shop – he would cut open a marrow or supersized courgette, stuff it with raisins, then hang it upside down and leave it to ferment for months. He said it made the most wonderful marrow brandy! We never did try it, but were always intrigued.

There are loads of different varieties of courgette besides the common green one, from yellow courgettes to grenade-type circular courgettes to the serpent-like Tromba courgette. Courgettes didn't really come on the scene until the 1920s. Originally cultivated around Milan, in Italy, they spread across Europe. In Ireland and the UK we call them 'courgette', which is the French word, but in North America the Italian word 'zucchini' is used, as it is believed that migrants brought them from their native Italy and started to cultivate them.

BUYING & STORING

You don't want great big courgettes, as these will be woody and tough. In Italy they often sell small young courgettes that have a slightly yellow inside, these are super-sweet and have a gentle nutty note to them. The skin ideally should be vibrant and glossy, and if the courgette has any blemishes, these are easy to cut out. Just ensure that the courgette is firm – you should not be able to bend it without snapping it. Courgettes will keep for at least a week in the fridge; they don't need to be stored in plastic or an airtight container.

GROWING

Courgettes are a summer veg and follow a growing season that's similar to tomatoes. They are usually planted in early spring, are very fast-growing, and are in season right through the summer from June onwards. The season typically finishes before any frosts in October.

Courgettes are fast and vigorous plants to grow in the garden. They have big leaves and need plenty of space. They love the heat and a maritime climate. If you go on holiday and there are small courgettes in your garden, you will likely return to big marrows in a matter of weeks!

Courgette flowers are also a real delicacy and rightly so – they are difficult to harvest and usually need to be used the same day that they are picked. They are hard to get hold of, so we've only eaten them a handful of times, but they are typically coated in a batter and deep-fried, or else stuffed with cheese and a cooked grain and then fried!

COOKING

As we mentioned already, courgettes are very high in water, so they do require a little longer to brown, but it is this browning or caramelizing that elevates their flavour. When roasting, try to make sure they are well spaced out so they have room to brown or slightly char. Similarly, when grilling, make sure your grill is nice and hot and that the courgettes are given time to cook to a melt-in-your-mouth texture and to develop some char lines.

One method that we have used a few times in this chapter is grating a courgette and adding salt to draw out some of the water, then adding this grated courgette to a batter to make a fritter, like the courgette fritters (page 186). In the case of the easy one-pan courgette pizza (page 197), we use both the separated courgette water and the grated courgette for a courgette pizza dough that tastes beautiful! You can grill them, as we have done in the epic charred courgette Reuben sandwich (page 188), barbecue them, sauté them as we did for the courgette and cherry tomato tarte Tatin (page 191), roast them as we did for the roasted courgette summer lasagne (page 198), and even add them to cakes for a sweet treat, like we have done in the courgette and lime cupcakes (page 199), along with lots more in this chapter.

NUTRITION

Courgettes are high in fibre and water and low in calories, so they are great to fill up on. They are not the most nutrient-dense of veg because of their high water content, but they do contain decent amounts of vitamin C and lots of fibre, which helps your immune system and digestion, along with potassium, which helps blood pressure and cardiovascular function.

The average courgette weighs 160g, so half a courgette counts as one of your 5-a-day.

Courgette Crêpes with Spinach and Ricotta

Creamy and delicious, these crêpes only take 20 minutes. They make a fabulous breakfast or brunch, or even a dinner! They're based on the traditional French savoury socca pancake, which is a chickpea pancake that's high in protein and really has an eggy, light, fluffy pancake texture. If you can't get gram flour, simply use plain white flour.

10 INGREDIENTS

1. 130g cashew nuts

2. ½ tsp garlic powder

3. juice of ½ a lemon

4. 100g spinach

5. 500g courgettes (approx. 2 courgettes)

6. 240g gram flour (chickpea flour), or plain white flour

7. 500ml veg stock

8. 4 tbsp ground flax seeds

9. 2 tsp baking powder

10. 1 red chilli

For the spinach ricotta, put the cashew nuts into a pan and cover with just-boiled water. Bring to the boil, then reduce to a simmer for 10 minutes. Drain and give them a good rinse.

Put the cashew nuts into a blender with the garlic powder, lemon juice, ½ teaspoon of salt, a pinch of black pepper and 100ml of water. Blend until super-smooth. If the mixture is a little lumpy, put it through a sieve to get a creamy sauce and keep the leftovers in the sieve to use as a nutty garnish for a salad or savoury dinner.

Put the spinach into a pan with 50ml of just-boiled water, then put the lid on and leave to wilt for 3 minutes until all the leaves have cooked down. Using a sieve over the sink, transfer the spinach and give it a good squeeze to remove any excess moisture. Roughly chop and put into a large bowl with the cashew ricotta. Then, gently fold them together. Taste and season with more salt, black pepper or lemon juice if it needs it.

To make the crêpe batter, finely grate the courgettes and put them into a sieve with a generous pinch of salt. Mix, then place the sieve over a bowl and leave while you prepare the rest of the ingredients.

Sieve the gram flour into a large bowl and add the veg stock, flax seeds, baking powder, a pinch of salt and the grated courgettes. Mix well until you have a nice homogeneous batter.

Heat a non-stick pan on a high heat. Once hot, spread 1 teaspoon of olive oil around the pan and reduce to a medium heat. Drop in a dollop of your crêpe batter and spread it out evenly so there is a thin coating in the pan. Leave to cook until it starts to bubble, forming little aeration pockets (you'll know what we mean when you are doing this!) and slightly browning along the edges.

Use a silicone spatula to turn the pancake and repeat on the other side. (The gram flour batter will hold its shape better; you will have to be more careful if using plain flour.) Repeat with the rest of your batter.

Finely slice the chilli. Top each pancake with a generous covering of the spinach ricotta and decorate with sliced red chilli.

COURGETTES

Courgette Fritters

These are easy to make and very tasty, with a lovely fresh lemon mint yoghurt dipping sauce. We usually serve them with a simple salad, brown rice or sauerkraut and a little avocado.

8 INGREDIENTS

1. 1 large to medium courgette

2. 1 small red chilli

3. ½ a bunch of spring onions

4. 1 x 400g tin of butter beans

5. 10g fresh mint or coriander

6. zest of 1 lemon, juice of ½

7. 85g plain white flour

8. 150ml coconut yoghurt, or non-dairy yoghurt of choice

Grate the courgette into a colander. Sprinkle with a pinch of salt, then squeeze in your hands for 30 seconds and leave to sit for about 5 minutes to lose moisture.

Meanwhile, finely chop the chilli (remove the seeds, if you don't like it spicy) and spring onions. Drain and rinse the butter beans. Finely chop the mint or coriander leaves and set a quarter of these aside.

After leaving the courgettes to sit for 5 minutes, squeeze all the juice out of them with your hands and discard the liquid. Place the courgettes in a large bowl. Add the drained butter beans and mash using a potato masher. Add the herbs, chilli, spring onions and lemon zest, and mix well. Add 1½ teaspoons of salt and ¼ teaspoon of black pepper, then taste and add more seasoning if needed.

Sieve in the flour and mix so it is fully incorporated.

Using your hands, take the equivalent of 2 tablespoons of the batter and roll them into 6 disc-shaped fritters. Put a non-stick pan on a high heat. Once hot, add ½ teaspoon of olive oil and spread around the pan. Gently wipe away the excess using some kitchen paper, then add the fritters and cook for a few minutes on each side until they are golden brown (approx. 5 minutes on each side). Repeat until they are all cooked.

Mix the yoghurt with the lemon juice, the reserved mint or coriander leaves, a pinch of salt and ground black pepper, to make a simple and delicious dipping sauce. Serve with the fritters.

Charred Courgette Reuben Sandwich

This is one of the most popular sandwiches in our café. It has all the components that make up an epic sandwich – it's crispy, gooey, chewy, sweet, acidic, creamy and so satisfying! Charlie May, a head baker with us, came up with this and it is such a magic sandwich, it's well worth the effort. Use store-bought barbecue sauce and vegan mayo to save time.

8 INGREDIENTS

1. 200g barbecue sauce (page 276)

2. 75g vegan mayo (page 275)

3. 100g tempeh or aubergine

4. 1 medium courgette

5. 4 slices of sourdough bread

6. 8 sliced gherkins

7. 100g red sauerkraut, or sauerkraut of choice

8. 2 slices of vegan Cheddar cheese

Preheat the oven to 200°C fan/220°C/gas 7. Line two baking trays with baking parchment.

Add 2 tablespoons of the barbecue sauce to the vegan mayo to make a quick-fire Russian-style mayonnaise and mix well. Set aside.

Slice the tempeh or aubergine into long thin strips, approx. ½cm thick. You should get around 8 slices of tempeh or 12 slices of aubergine. Slice the courgette into thin strips, approx. ½cm thick.

Spread the courgette slices on one of the baking trays and mix with 1 tablespoon of olive oil and a generous pinch of salt. Put the tempeh or aubergine strips on the second baking tray, coat them with the rest of the barbecue sauce and spread them out in an even layer.

Bake both trays of veg strips in the oven for 12 minutes, with no need to turn. Take out the tempeh or aubergine and set aside. Carefully turn the courgette slices and bake for a further 10 minutes. Remove and leave to cool.

To assemble this epic sandwich, add a generous dollop of the barbecue mayo and Russian-style mayo to each slice of bread. On one slice, add a layer of courgette slices, approx. 4 per sandwich, followed by a layer of tempeh or aubergine (approx. 6 per sandwich). Then add a layer of sliced gherkins, then a layer of sauerkraut and finally a layer of vegan Cheddar. Top with the other slice of bread.

Either eat cool, as it is, or grill for 10 minutes, so that the cheese melts and the bread goes crispy!

Courgette Tagliatelle with Avocado Mash, Cherry Tomatoes and Toasted Chickpeas

This dish is lovely served with toasted bread rubbed with garlic and a little olive oil. It's best eaten fresh, as otherwise the courgette can go soft and mushy. A lovely light satisfying summer dish, great on hotter days or for dinners in the garden.

10 INGREDIENTS

1. 3 courgettes
2. juice of 1 lemon
3. 1 x 400g tin of chickpeas
4. a pinch of cayenne or chilli pepper
5. 1 tsp paprika
6. 1 tbsp nutritional yeast
7. 1 tbsp tamari or soy sauce
8. 2 ripe avocados
9. a handful of rocket or other salad greens
10. 15 cherry tomatoes

Preheat the oven to 180°C fan/200°C/gas 6. Line two baking trays with baking parchment.

Using a wide vegetable peeler, 'peel' two of the courgettes into long thin strips. Stack the strips on top of each other and slice them in half lengthways into tagliatelle-sized strips (approx. 6mm). Keep the ends of the courgettes that you can't peel – we will use them later.

Put the courgette strips into a mixing bowl, separating them as you add them. Add half the lemon juice and a generous pinch of salt, then mix well and massage the courgette tagliatelle for a minute or two. Set aside.

Cut the remaining whole courgette and the leftover courgette pieces from peeling into bite-size pieces, and put them on one of the lined baking trays. Toss them with 1 teaspoon of olive oil and a small pinch of salt.

Drain and rinse the chickpeas and put them into a bowl. Add the cayenne, paprika, nutritional yeast and tamari, along with 1 tablespoon of olive oil and a pinch of salt. Mix well, doing your best to coat the chickpeas evenly. Transfer these coated chickpeas to the second lined baking tray.

Put the trays of courgettes and chickpeas into the oven. Bake the courgettes for 18 minutes, and bake the chickpeas for 25 minutes, until crispy.

Cut the avocados in half, remove the stones, then scoop out the flesh with a spoon and chop it into small pieces. Place in a bowl with the rest of the lemon juice, a decent pinch of salt and a pinch of black pepper, and roughly mash together with a fork.

Remove any excess water from the courgette tagliatelle by giving them a light squeeze. Add the mashed avocado to the courgette tagliatelle, along with the rocket, and mix together gently. Divide the mixture between two bowls or plates. Slice the cherry tomatoes in half and sprinkle on top of each serving.

Remove the toasted chickpeas and courgettes from the oven and leave to cool for 5 minutes, then place a good handful of both on top of each of the dishes for added flavour and a lovely contrast of texture and spice. The rest of the toasted spiced chickpeas will keep for a couple of weeks in an airtight container in the fridge.

SERVES 2   TAKES 40 minutes

11/22

Courgette and Cherry Tomato Tarte Tatin

This isn't something that could sit for long,

A really easy one-pan summer tarte Tatin that tastes every bit as good as it looks. Our kids thought it tasted like a puff pastry pizza. The recipe is easy to adapt to other veg – just make sure they're fast-cooking.

before going soggy & flat

9 INGREDIENTS

1. 1 x 320g sheet of vegan ready-rolled puff pastry *300/8*
2. 1 medium courgette
3. 1 red onion
4. 2 cloves of garlic
5. 300g cherry tomatoes
6. 2 tbsp balsamic vinegar
7. 1 tbsp maple syrup *55*
8. 1 tbsp tamari or soy sauce
9. a few sprigs of fresh thyme

If you are using frozen puff pastry, ensure it is properly thawed first.

Preheat the oven to 180°C fan/200°C/gas 6. Line a medium baking tray (approx. 25 x 18cm) with baking parchment.

Slice the courgette into ½cm rounds. Peel and finely slice the red onion and garlic. Halve the cherry tomatoes. Put a large wide-bottomed frying pan on a medium heat. Once hot, add 1 tablespoon of olive oil along with the courgette and red onion and fry for about 5–10 minutes, stirring regularly, until the veg start to char. Add the tomato halves and garlic and fry for another 5 minutes.

In a bowl, whisk together the balsamic vinegar, maple syrup and tamari. Add to the veg and leave to reduce for a further 3 minutes. Remove from the heat and allow to cool slightly.

Strip the thyme leaves from the sprigs and stir half of them into the veg mixture. Transfer the cooked veg to the lined baking tray and spread out evenly. Carefully place the puff pastry sheet on top, tucking in any edges (if your tray is smaller than the puff pastry sheet you will need to cut it slightly). Bake in the oven for 20 minutes, until the pastry starts to turn golden.

Remove the dish from the oven. Put a board that is slightly bigger than the baking tray on top of it and carefully flip, so that the pastry is now on the bottom and the cooked veg on top. Garnish with the remaining thyme leaves, slice and enjoy!

60 oel

used 2 sheets Puff Pastry

4 15 / 8

It may have been better w/plain tomatoes w/o maple w/o sweetness

COURGETTES

Courgette Ravioli with Homemade Feta and Sweet Tomato Sauce

When Steve first had this idea it seemed a little strange, but it actually worked out beautifully and saved having to make fresh pasta. This is a great simple meal for all the family – a winner with kids, and it's a good way to get them to eat more veg, as they will never notice the courgette with our creamy vegan feta in the ravioli filling and the lovely sweet tomato sauce! We like to serve this with fresh basil leaves and a sprinkling of nutritional yeast.

10 INGREDIENTS

1. 100g cashew nuts
2. 3 tbsp non-dairy milk
3. 1 tbsp lemon juice
4. 450g dried white lasagne sheets
5. 1 medium courgette, approx. 200g
6. 1 x 400g tin of cooked lentils
7. 2 cloves of garlic
8. 1 x 400g tin of chopped tomatoes
9. 100g tomato purée
10. 2 tbsp maple syrup

To make the cashew feta, put the cashew nuts into a bowl, pour over boiling water to cover, and leave for 10 minutes, or overnight if you have time. Then drain and rinse the cashews and put them into a blender with the milk, lemon juice and ⅓ teaspoon of salt. Blend until smooth, to make cashew feta. Set aside.

Soak the lasagne sheets in boiling water for 5–10 minutes, until soft. Four baking trays, or large bowls or dishes, work well for this, so you can soak the lasagne sheets in an even layer without them overlapping and sticking together. When softened, drain and rinse in cold water, then toss in 1 tablespoon of olive oil and set aside.

Grate the courgette and add a pinch of salt, then leave to sit for 5 minutes in a sieve over a bowl to catch any water. Then press the courgette into the sieve with a spoon to squeeze out the last of the liquid. Put the drained courgette into a bowl. Add the cashew feta to the bowl of grated courgette and mix well.

To fill the ravioli, take one lasagne sheet at a time and cut it in half. Add 1 heaped teaspoon of filling to the centre of one side of each half sheet. Cover with the other half sheet and seal the filling inside the ravioli. Press firmly around the edges, keeping the filling in the centre. Repeat with the rest of the lasagne sheets and filling, then chill in the fridge for 10 minutes while you make your sauce.

Drain and rinse the lentils. Peel and finely dice the garlic. Put 1 tablespoon of olive oil into a medium to large pan over a high heat, and when hot add the garlic. Cook for a minute or until it starts to turn golden, stirring occasionally so it does not burn. Add the drained lentils, chopped tomatoes, tomato purée, maple syrup, ¾ teaspoon of salt and a pinch of black pepper, and mix well. Simmer for 10 minutes.

To cook the ravioli, fill a large saucepan with water, add ½ tablespoon of salt and bring to the boil, then lower to a simmer. When your sauce is nearly ready, add the prepared ravioli to the simmering water. Cook for 3–4 minutes, then drain and add directly to the sauce. Toss all the cooked ravioli gently in the sauce and divide between the plates.

Easy One-pan Courgette Pizza

A quick one-pan, no-proofing pizza. Here we use the courgette liquid in the base and the drier flesh as a topping. This is a real treat!

8 INGREDIENTS

1. 150g courgettes (approx. 1 courgette)

2. 250g self-raising flour

3. 1 small red onion

4. 1 small red pepper

5. ½ red chilli

6. 2 fresh or defrosted vegan sausages

7. 2 tbsp tomato purée

8. 2 tbsp pesto of choice (see page 273)

Preheat the oven to 250°C fan or the highest temperature on a conventional or gas oven.

Grate the courgettes. Then, using your hands, squeeze the grated courgette one handful at a time over a bowl, to extract all the liquid. Leave the squeezed courgette aside, to use for the topping of the pizza, and keep the liquid in the bowl.

To make your dough, put the flour into a mixing bowl. Pour the courgette liquid into a jug (you should have about 65ml), add a small pinch of salt, then add water to reach a total of 125ml. Add this liquid to the flour and bring together into a rough dough. The dough will look slightly green, but don't worry, this will cook out. Transfer it to a lightly floured surface and knead for 5–10 minutes, until it forms a nice elastic dough, smooth to the touch. You could alternatively use a stand mixer with a dough hook for 4–5 minutes. Shape the dough into a round, cover with the upturned mixing bowl and leave to relax while you prepare the toppings.

Peel and halve the red onion and slice into half-moons. Cut the red pepper into strips. Finely slice the red chilli, removing the seeds if you prefer it less spicy. Cut the vegan sausages into 7 slices each.

Put a large (approx. 30cm) ovenproof frying pan on a high heat. Once hot, add 1 tablespoon of olive oil and all the prepared veg including the grated courgette (about 100g), and the sliced vegan sausages. Add a generous pinch of salt and cook for 7–10 minutes, until the onion and courgette are softened and the sausages are nicely charred. Remove the toppings from the pan to a bowl and wipe the frying pan clean with kitchen paper.

Mix the tomato purée and pesto together in a bowl.

Take your dough from under the mixing bowl and place it on a lightly floured work surface. By hand, flatten, stretch and shape the dough to roughly the size of your frying pan, ensuring that the dough is thinner in the middle than at the edge. Heat the empty frying pan over a medium heat and add 1 teaspoon of oil, then carefully add the dough to the pan, pushing it to the edges to cover the bottom of the pan if you need to. Working quickly, spread the sauce in an even layer over the dough, leaving 1cm around the edges for the crust, then scatter your cooked toppings over the sauce. Cook over the heat for 4–5 minutes, just until the base is nicely browned and starts to firm up. Then transfer to the oven for 8–10 minutes, until the edges of the pizza are golden. Remove from the oven – the handle will be very hot. Enjoy!

COURGETTES

8/22

SERVES 6   TAKES 1 hour 20 minutes

Roasted Courgette Summer Lasagne

A delicious white lasagne, this is a summer delight that has a lovely note of mint and lemon to cut through the creamy sauce. It's a real crowd-pleaser if you have people coming around. Serve with a simple green salad and some garlic bread.

500 – oil

10 INGREDIENTS

1. 2 medium courgettes, approx. 500g

2. 600g sweet potatoes

150

3. 100g frozen peas   50/10

4. 15g mint, leaves only, finely chopped

5. 75g vegan Cheddar cheese, plus extra for the topping

100/2

6. 9 tbsp white flour

100/2

7. 1 litre oat milk or plant milk of choice

60/4

8. zest and juice of 1 lemon

9. 100g baby spinach

30/10

10. 300g lasagne sheets

300/10

Preheat the oven to 220°C fan/240°C/gas 9.

Cut the courgettes into ½cm rounds. Cut the sweet potatoes into ½cm slices. Put the frozen peas into a bowl, cover with boiling water and leave to thaw. Pick the leaves off the mint sprigs and finely chop them. Grate the vegan Cheddar.

Put the courgettes on one lined baking tray and the sweet potatoes on another. Add ½ tablespoon of oil and a generous pinch of salt to each tray, and mix well. Bake in the oven for 20 minutes, until the veg start to brown up around the edges, then remove and reduce the oven temperature to 180°C fan/200°C/gas 6.

To make the béchamel sauce, put 9 tablespoons of olive oil into a pan on a medium heat. Once hot, sieve in the flour and cook for 1–2 minutes, stirring continuously with a whisk until it goes slightly golden. Slowly add the oat milk, stirring continuously. Bring to the boil, then reduce to a gentle simmer, stirring to be careful that nothing sticks to the bottom. Once simmering, and when it reaches a creamy texture, remove from the heat. Add 1 teaspoon of salt, a pinch of ground black pepper, the lemon zest and juice, and mix in the vegan Cheddar. Taste and adjust the seasoning if it needs it.

Put a thin layer of béchamel along the bottom of a deep ovenproof dish or tray approx. 30 x 22cm, and spread it out evenly. Remove one-third of the béchamel (approx. 300g) from the pan and set aside.

In a large bowl, mix together the cooked sweet potato and courgette, peas, baby spinach and chopped mint, along with the rest of the béchamel, and gently mix. Taste and adjust the seasoning to your liking.

Now you can start layering it up. On top of the layer of béchamel in the dish, make a layer of lasagne sheets. Cover them with half the veg and béchamel mix, and spread it out evenly. Cover that with another layer of lasagne sheets, and the rest of the veg. Finish with a final layer of sheets and spread the reserved béchamel over the final layer. Sprinkle with more vegan cheese and bake for 25 minutes, until the pasta is cooked.

To test, simply insert a knife or skewer and it should pass through the pasta indicating that it's cooked. If it's not ready, just turn the heat down to prevent the top browning too much and leave to cook until the pasta is soft.

100 hour/2

1300/26

Courgette and Lime Cupcakes

This is a really fun recipe to make with courgettes. These delicious, elegant cupcakes are topped with a lovely lime icing, the zingy cream-cheese frosting balancing out the sweetness of the cakes to give a treat that is neither too sweet nor too acidic.

7 INGREDIENTS

1. 100g courgettes

2. 300g self-raising flour

3. 200g coconut sugar or caster sugar

4. 250ml non-dairy milk

5. zest and juice of 3 limes

6. 450g vegan cream cheese

7. 150g icing sugar

Preheat the oven to 180°C fan/200°C/gas 6. Line a muffin tray with paper cases.

Coarsely grate the courgettes. Sift the flour and sugar into a medium to large mixing bowl and mix well.

Put the milk into a jug with the zest and juice of 2 limes and 100ml of sunflower oil. Mix and allow the milk to curdle for a few minutes. Make a well in the centre of the dry ingredients and pour in the curdled milk. Bring together using a spatula until all the ingredients are combined.

Fold the grated courgette through the batter. Pour the batter into each muffin case, no more than three-quarters full. Bake in the oven for 20–25 minutes, rotating halfway through the cooking time.

Remove the cupcakes from the oven when they have risen and check that they are done by inserting a clean skewer into the centre – if the skewer comes out clean they are done; if not, put the cupcakes back into the oven for another 5 minutes or so. Allow to cool fully before icing.

For the icing, put the vegan cream cheese into a mixing bowl and use a whisk to break it up until smooth and creamy. Sieve in the icing sugar and juice of the remaining lime plus most of the zest. Whisk until smooth. Pop back into the fridge until you are ready to ice the cupcakes.

Simply frost each cupcake using a palette knife or a spatula. If you want pretty swirls, half fill a piping bag with a large star nozzle, or use a large freezer/sandwich bag and snip about 1cm off one of the corners, and pipe a nice swirl on to each cupcake. Decorate with the rest of the lime zest.

COURGETTES

MAKES 8–10 slices **TAKES** 1 hour 20 minutes

Courgette and Lemon Loaf Cake with a Lemon Curd

When Dave's daughters, Elsie and Izzy, first tried this, they thought there was no way there was courgette in it! The idea of courgette in cake might sound a little unusual, but this cake is zesty, moist and delicious, as well as quick to make. Decorate with fresh or frozen berries or some lemon zest.

10 INGREDIENTS

1. 2 tbsp ground flax seed
2. 100g courgettes
3. 300g self-raising flour
4. 400g caster sugar
5. 200ml sunflower oil
6. zest and juice of 2 lemons
7. 1 tsp vanilla extract
8. 400ml oat milk, or non-dairy milk of choice
9. 75g vegan block butter
10. 3 tbsp cornflour

Preheat the oven to 180°C fan/200°C/gas 6. Line a 900g loaf tin with baking parchment.

To make your flax egg, mix the ground flax seed with 6 tablespoons of water until well incorporated, then set aside for 3–5 minutes to thicken.

Coarsely grate the courgettes. Sieve the self-raising flour and 300g of sugar into a large bowl and mix well. In a separate bowl, mix the sunflower oil, the zest and juice of 1 lemon, the grated courgette, flax egg, vanilla extract and 150ml of oat milk and combine. Make a well in the centre of the dry ingredients and add the wet ingredients. Mix well so they are incorporated, while also being careful not to over-mix so it doesn't develop any gluten.

Pour the batter into the lined tin and bake for 55 minutes, or until a skewer comes out clean. Rotate the tin halfway through, so the loaf has an even colour. Remove from the oven and leave in the tin to cool fully.

For the curd, melt the vegan butter in a small to medium pan over a low heat. Add 250ml of non-dairy milk and the juice of the second lemon and sieve in 100g of sugar. Simmer until the sugar has dissolved.

Sieve in the cornflour and whisk continuously while simmering for 3–4 minutes, until the curd has thickened. Don't be tempted to add more cornflour, as it will thicken on cooling. Stir in the lemon zest.

Transfer to a bowl and cover with cling film so it is touching and covering the surface of the curd. This will prevent a skin forming. Allow to cool fully in the fridge for 30 minutes, then whisk and serve with the courgette loaf.

Once the loaf cake has fully cooled, remove from the tin. Put a generous dollop of lemon curd on top and decorate with some berries or citrus zest.

№ 8

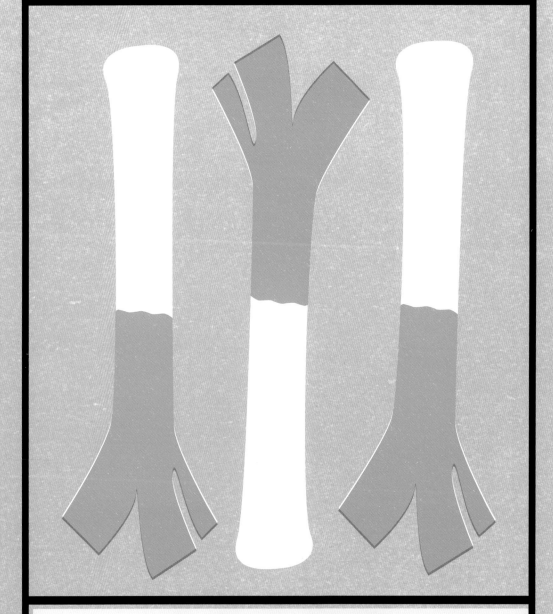

LEEKS

This is one of our all-time favourite veg and a definite unsung hero when compared to kale and others.

Anywhere you would use an onion, you can replace it with a leek. Pungent and potent when raw, leeks turn incredibly sweet when cooked, especially baked, when they become succulent and melt-in-your-mouth delicious! They are rarely the star of a dish but are an essential ingredient in so many recipes. We often use them in stocks and soups as base ingredients, as they give a beautiful depth of flavour.

When we were growing up in Ireland, generally just the white part of the leek was used and the green part discarded. It was only when a friend from the Basque Country, Borja, was working with us in the kitchen and said that back home they only ate the green part of the leek and discarded the white part, as the green was the most nutritious – it was then that we started to use the whole of the leek. The white part is generally juicier and succulent, and the green leafy part is more fibrous, but once cooked down the green part becomes soft and tender. Often sediment can hide in the green parts of the leek, so give them a good wash before using. Use the full length of the leek, including the green parts, to add more nutrition and flavour to your dishes.

Leeks are part of the onion family, otherwise known as alliums, alongside garlic, onion and spring onions. They have the unmistakable smell and sharpness of an onion but are far milder. The Romans believed leeks to be superior to onions, which they felt were only fit for the poor. Legend has it that when a Welsh king was due to fight a battle with the incoming Saxons, he ordered his men to wear leeks on their hats in order to tell friend from foe. The Welsh were victorious and adopted the leek as one of the national emblems of Wales.

LEEKS

BUYING & STORING

Leeks come in various sizes – ideally the main thing you are looking for is that the leaves or green part are still vibrant, and that the leek is not woody or dry, as this means it will have lost its juiciness and much of its flavour. They store well in the fridge or in a dark cool cupboard.

GROWING

Leeks are in season from July right through the winter to May. In March, when the spring warmth begins, they start to bolt – in March and April they tend to be sweet and tender, but by May, the end of the leek-growing season, they can often be bitter, hard and yellow.

Leeks are best planted during the cooler weather of spring and autumn. They grow well in raised beds or containers. Ideally space leeks about 15cm apart in an area that gets approximately 6 hours of sun daily and has well-drained and nutrient-rich soil. Harvest leeks any time once they are large enough to eat.

We have grown leek micro greens on our sprout farm for years, and although they take longer to sprout, they have an incredible pungent taste. We add them to toasties to give a pop of flavour.

COOKING

Leeks tend to harbour lots of dirt and sand, so rinse them well under the cold tap or soak them in cold water to remove any sediment. We like to use the full length of the leek, the green and the white parts, as each brings a slightly different flavour and texture. Leeks can be steamed, fried as we have done in the leek, cashew and celeriac soup with leek frizzles (page 207), roasted like we did in the sweet miso leek pastry parcels with avocado mash (page 210), stir-fried as in the Mexican leek and cheese toastie (page 219), sautéed as we did in the leek, red onion and vegan feta quiche (page 214), and even eaten raw (we decided not to include any raw leek recipes!). They are one of the most succulent and versatile veg, so we hope these dishes inspire you to cook with them more often.

NUTRITION

As with most of the veg in this book, leeks are high in vitamin C and A, both important for a healthy immune system and good for eyesight in dim light, and they are packed with fibre, minerals and antioxidants. There are also multiple studies now linking vegetables from the allium family, like leeks, to a lower risk of heart disease and stroke. While most of these studies have tested onions and garlic, leeks contain several of the same beneficial compounds, thought to lower inflammation and protect heart health.

Like all veg, leeks are a good source of fibre and water, which may prevent hunger, promote feelings of fullness and help you naturally eat less. The average leek weighs about 250g, so roughly one-third of a leek, or 80g, is considered one of your 5-a-day.

Leek, Cashew and Celeriac Soup with Leek Frizzles

A super-hearty, nourishing and simple-to-make soup that is like a hug on a cold winter's evening. We use celeriac, which is a starchy root veg, part of the celery family; it functions very like a potato, so if you can't source celeriac just use potato instead.

7 INGREDIENTS

1. 600g leeks (approx. 2 large)
2. 3 cloves of garlic
3. 600g celeriac or potatoes
4. 2 litres veg stock
5. 75g baby spinach
6. juice of ½ a lemon
7. 150g cashew nuts

Finely slice the leeks, including the green parts, into rounds and give them a good wash. Peel and finely chop the garlic. Chop the celeriac into bite-size pieces.

Heat 1 tablespoon of olive oil in a large wide-bottomed pan on a high heat. Add half the leeks and cook for 4 minutes, stirring regularly. Add the garlic and cook for a further minute, then add the celeriac and 1 teaspoon of salt. Cook for a further 4 minutes, stirring regularly. Put a lid on the pan, turn the heat down to medium, and cook for a further 10 minutes, stirring occasionally.

Add the veg stock and spinach and bring to the boil. Reduce the heat to medium and leave the soup simmering away for a further 5 minutes. Add the lemon juice, 1½ teaspoons of salt and ¾ teaspoon of black pepper, and stir well.

While the soup is simmering, toast the cashew nuts in a small dry pan over a medium heat. They should start to turn golden after about 5 or 6 minutes. Remove from the heat and set aside a quarter of the toasted nuts to use as a garnish. Add the rest to the soup.

Take the soup from the heat and blend with an immersion/stick blender or in an upright blender until smooth. Taste and add more salt and pepper if it needs it.

For the frizzles, heat 1 tablespoon of oil in a small pan over a medium heat. Once hot, add the remaining chopped leek and cook for 4–5 minutes, stirring occasionally, until nicely browned and a little charred. Roughly chop the rest of the cashew nuts.

Serve the soup in bowls, topped with the leek frizzles and toasted cashew nuts.

LEEKS

Roasted Leek, Black Bean, Sweet Potato and Feta Bowl

The combination of a homemade vegan feta, roasted veg and beans in this recipe makes an epic dinner or side dish. We serve this in a bowl, and the sweetness of roasted leeks with the creamy feta and satisfying black beans means every bite hits the spot! Serve with corn chips to make a lovely sharing bowl.

10 INGREDIENTS

1. 60g cashew nuts
2. 300g firm tofu
3. juice of 3 lemons
4. 2 tbsp nutritional yeast
5. 2 large leeks
6. 500g sweet potatoes
7. 1 red pepper
8. 1 x 400g tin of black beans
9. 3 ripe avocados
10. corn chips and chilli flakes to serve (optional)

Preheat the oven to 200°C fan/220°C/gas 7.

To make the vegan feta, simmer the cashew nuts in a pan of boiling water for 10 minutes to soften them. Drain and rinse the nuts and put them into a food processor with the tofu, 60ml of olive oil, the juice of 1 lemon, the nutritional yeast and 1 teaspoon of salt. Blend until smooth.

Chop the leeks, including the green parts, into 2–3cm chunks and give them a good wash. Cut the sweet potatoes and red pepper into bite-size pieces. Drain and rinse the black beans.

Put the prepared sweet potato, leek and red pepper into a large mixing bowl. Toss in 2 tablespoons of olive oil and 1 teaspoon of salt. Spread evenly on two baking trays, giving them lots of space, and bake for 30 minutes.

When the veg are cooked, put them into a mixing bowl with the drained black beans and the juice of 1 lemon. Mix well. Add the vegan feta to the bowl and gently mix to coat the veg.

Cut the avocados in half and remove the stones. Spoon out the flesh on to a chopping board, chop it into cubes and put them into a bowl. Add the juice of the remaining lemon, a good pinch of salt and a pinch of black pepper. Mix well, trying to leave plenty of texture. You are not looking for mashed avocado.

Transfer everything to a large serving bowl, add the avocado in the centre and serve with corn chips and a sprinkle of chilli flakes if you like a little heat.

Sweet Miso Leek Pastry Parcels with Avocado Mash

This may sound complex and bizarre to you, but bear with us. This is one of Steve's favourite ways to eat leeks. Leek is a subtly sweet veg and, when cooked well, it is juicy and melts in your mouth. This is like a Japanese-inspired leek pastry roll, with a magnificent dipping sauce! It makes a fab brunch, lunch, starter or accompaniment to dinner.

10 INGREDIENTS

1. 3 medium leeks (800g)

2. 2 tbsp brown rice miso paste

3. 2 tbsp maple syrup

4. 1 tsp smoked paprika

5. 1½ tbsp tomato purée

6. juice of 1 lemon

7. 1 x 320g sheet of vegan ready-rolled puff pastry

8. 2 tbsp oat milk or non-dairy milk of choice

9. 10g fresh coriander

10. 1 avocado

Preheat the oven to 200°C fan/220°C/gas 7.

Cut the leeks into 6–8cm lengths, including the green parts, and give them a good wash. Put them into a bowl and mix with 2 tablespoons of olive oil and a generous pinch of salt. Lay them on a baking tray in a single layer and bake for 15 minutes.

Mix together the miso, maple syrup, smoked paprika, tomato purée, half the lemon juice and 3 tablespoons of water to make the sauce.

Remove the baked leeks from the oven. Add half the sauce to them, reserving the rest for serving, and mix to coat evenly. Bake for a further 5–10 minutes. Remove from the oven and set aside to cool.

Roll out the sheet of pastry on a lightly floured surface and divide it into 9 even rectangles approx. 8 x 12cm (cut the sheet in thirds lengthways and then again into thirds horizontally and this will give you 9 squares). Place a baked leek on each rectangle, along with some of the sauce, and roll them up in the pastry. Turn the leek rolls seam side down and press down on them with the palm of your hand to help seal them firmly and to ensure they stay rolled when you bake them. Press or crimp the open ends of the rolls, using a fork, or just press together until sealed. Repeat with the remaining leeks and pastry, until they are all rolled, and place on a lined baking tray ensuring they are well spaced out and not touching.

Using a pastry brush, brush each parcel with oat milk. Bake for 20 minutes until the pastry is lovely and golden.

To make the avocado mash, chop the fresh coriander. Halve the avocado and remove the stone. Chop the flesh roughly and put it into a bowl with the coriander, a good pinch of salt, a small pinch of black pepper and the rest of the lemon juice. Mash well until smooth.

Remove the leek rolls from the oven. Just before serving, drizzle over the rest of the miso sauce and serve with a nice dollop of avocado mash on the side.

SERVES 4   **TAKES** 25 minutes

Easy Leek and Butter Bean Burritos with Guacamole

This is a great family favourite in Dave's house – his kids love it and it's easy to make. It is a wonderful sharing dinner where everyone can get stuck in.

10 INGREDIENTS
1. 4 vegan sausages
2. 2 leeks
3. 1 medium carrot
4. 1 small red chilli
5. 300g cherry tomatoes
6. 1 x 400g tin of butter beans
7. 20g fresh coriander
8. 3 ripe avocados
9. juice of 2 limes
10. 4 large wholemeal wraps

Thaw the vegan sausages if you are using frozen.

Slice the leeks, including the green parts, into 1cm rounds and give them a good wash. Grate the carrot. Finely chop the red chilli, omitting the seeds if you don't like too much spice. Halve the cherry tomatoes. Cut the vegan sausages into bite-size pieces. Drain and rinse the butter beans. Chop the coriander (including the stalks).

Put a wide-bottomed non-stick pan on a high heat. Once hot, add 1 tablespoon of olive oil and the vegan sausages. Fry for 4–5 minutes, stirring occasionally so they don't stick. Once they have started to turn brown, remove them from the pan and set aside.

In the same pan, heat ½ tablespoon of oil and add the chopped leek, grated carrot, chilli, cherry tomatoes and a good pinch of salt. Cook for 3 minutes, stirring regularly. Turn the heat down to low–medium, put a lid on the pan and allow the veg to steam in their own juices for about 8–10 minutes, stirring occasionally.

Meanwhile, make the guacamole. Cut the avocados in half, remove the stones, using a spoon, then spoon out the flesh on to a board and finely chop it. Put it into a bowl and add the juice of 1 lime, a quarter of the coriander, ½ teaspoon of salt and a good pinch of black pepper. Using a fork, mash the avocado until well mixed and it has reached your desired texture.

Add the butter beans and the vegan sausages to the cooked leek mixture, with 1 teaspoon of salt and a good pinch of black pepper. Cook on a medium heat, stirring occasionally, for 2–3 minutes until the butter beans are heated through. Mix in the rest of the coriander and the juice of the second lime.

Put a dry pan on a high heat. Once hot, heat a wrap until it starts to toast, about 2 minutes. Turn and repeat on the other side. Repeat with the remaining three wraps.

Serve the leek/butter bean mixture, guacamole and wraps in the middle of the table for everyone to make up their own burritos.

Leek, Red Onion and Vegan Feta Quiche

A lovely crispy pastry is filled with sweet leek and vegan feta, and topped with an egg-like quiche filling and some pine nuts. If you have any black sulphur salt (also known as kala namak), this goes great sprinkled over as you serve, as it gives that lovely egg-like taste to the quiche. It can be bought online.

10 INGREDIENTS

1. 1 x 320g sheet of vegan shortcrust pastry

2. 1 large leek, approx. 300g

3. 2 red onions

4. 75g vegan feta cheese

5. 6 cherry tomatoes

6. 300g silken tofu

7. 2 tbsp cornflour

8. ¼ tsp ground turmeric

9. 2 tsp garlic powder

10. 20g pine nuts

Thaw your pastry if using frozen. Preheat the oven to 200°C fan/220°C/gas 7.

Lightly oil your dish, ideally a quiche dish approx. 24cm diameter and 3cm depth, so that the quiche will come out easily after baking.

Using a rolling pin, on a lightly floured work surface, roll the pastry to fit the pie dish with about 1cm extra all round. Fit the pastry into the pie dish, ensuring that you spread it to the edges and leave sufficient overhang at the sides so that it won't shrink during baking. Trim any long overhanging pastry so it is even all the way round. Use a fork to prick the bottom of the pastry a few times to ensure no air pockets form.

To 'blind bake' the pastry, put a sheet of baking parchment on top of the pastry and top with dried beans. Bake in the oven for 10 minutes, then remove the baking parchment and beans and bake for a further 3–4 minutes to crisp up the base. Remove from the oven and set aside. Turn the oven temperature down to 180°C fan/200°C/gas 6.

Slice the leek into thin rounds, including the green parts, and give them a good wash. Peel and finely slice the red onions. Dice the vegan feta cheese. Halve the cherry tomatoes.

Heat 1 tablespoon of olive oil in a wide-bottomed non-stick pan on a high heat. Once hot, add the leeks, onions and a good pinch of salt. Cook for 4–5 minutes, stirring regularly, then turn the heat down to medium, put a lid on the pan and cook for a further 5 minutes, so that the veg cook in their own juices. Turn the heat off and leave to cool for a few minutes.

Put the tofu, cornflour, turmeric and garlic powder into a food processor with 1 teaspoon of salt and ½ teaspoon of black pepper. Blend until smooth.

In a large bowl, mix the tofu mixture with the cooled onion and leeks. Scatter the vegan feta in an even layer on the base of the tart shell, then spread the filling in an even layer over the feta. Place the cherry tomato halves, cut side up, on top and bake in the oven for 25 minutes. While it's baking, fry the pine nuts in a dry pan for 5 minutes until golden.

Remove the quiche from the oven and leave it to sit for 5–10 minutes before slicing. Sprinkle over the toasted pine nuts and black sulphur salt, if you have it.

Creamy Lemon, Leek and Caper Tagliatelle

Quick to make, super-satisfying and creamy, this lovely dish shows the versatility of leeks. Crispy capers are so good and add an irresistible, salty, chewy topping. This is a really light summer meal that goes perfectly eaten outside on a sunny day or evening.

10 INGREDIENTS

1. 4 tbsp capers

2. 100g frozen peas

3. 2 medium leeks

4. 1 clove of garlic

5. 15g fresh mint (or parsley) leaves

6. 200g dried tagliatelle

7. zest and juice of 1 lemon

8. 2 tbsp plain white flour

9. 200ml oat milk or non-dairy milk of choice

10. 1 tsp mustard

Rinse the capers and pat them dry. Thaw the frozen peas by pouring boiling water over them in a bowl and letting them sit. Finely slice the leeks, including the green parts, and give them a good wash. Peel and finely chop the garlic. Finely chop the mint leaves.

Bring a saucepan of water to the boil. Add 1 teaspoon of salt and the tagliatelle and cook as per the packet instructions. Drain the pasta and rinse in cold water to remove any excess starch and avoid it sticking together.

While the pasta is cooking, heat a large non-stick frying pan on a high heat. Once hot, add 1 tablespoon of olive oil and the capers. Cook for 5–6 minutes, until nice and crispy, stirring regularly. Remove and set aside for garnish.

In the same frying pan, heat a tablespoon of oil over a medium heat. Once hot, add the sliced leeks and cook for 4 minutes, stirring regularly. Add a pinch of salt and black pepper and 1 tablespoon of water, then put the lid on and cook for a further 4 minutes. This will encourage steaming and help the leeks become more succulent. Add the garlic and the lemon juice. Mix well and cook for a further 1–2 minutes without the lid.

To make the sauce, use the same pot you cooked the pasta in and put it on a high heat. Once hot, add 2 tablespoons of oil and allow to heat up, then sieve in the flour. Whisk together and cook for 1 minute, stirring constantly. Slowly add the oat milk, stirring constantly, then add the mustard, lemon zest, a generous pinch of salt and a pinch of black pepper. Bring to the boil, then reduce the heat and simmer for a further 4–5 minutes, continuously whisking until it starts to thicken. Remove from the heat.

To bring the dish together, drain the peas and add them to the pan of leeks, then add the cooked pasta and the sauce and warm through on a medium heat, allowing the flavours to combine. Add the chopped mint leaves, then taste and add more salt and pepper if it needs it.

Divide between bowls and serve with a sprinkling of crispy capers.

Super Green Spanakopita

Here is the classic Greek filo pastry bake with greens and vegan feta, done with 10 easy ingredients. This was a total hit with Steve's kids. It's crispy, creamy and makes a fab family dinner and a lovely cold lunch the next day. We make our own vegan feta here, which works really well.

10 INGREDIENTS

1. 7 sheets of filo pastry

2. 60g cashew nuts

3. 3 large leeks, approx. 600g

4. 2 cloves of garlic

5. 20g fresh mint leaves

6. 500g frozen spinach

7. juice of 2 lemons

8. 300g firm tofu, crumbled

9. 1 tsp garlic powder

10. 2 tbsp nutritional yeast

Thaw your filo pastry if using frozen. Preheat the oven to 180°C fan/200°C/gas 6.

Put the cashew nuts into a small saucepan, cover them with boiling water and simmer for 10 minutes to soften. Drain and set aside.

Slice the leeks into 1cm rounds, including the green parts, and give them a good wash. Peel and finely chop the garlic and finely chop the mint leaves.

Heat 1 tablespoon of olive oil in a wide-bottomed non-stick pan on a high heat. Once hot, add the leeks and a pinch of salt and cook for 5 minutes, stirring regularly. Add the garlic and cook for a further minute. Turn the heat down to medium and add the frozen spinach. Put a lid on the pan and cook for a further 5 minutes, then remove the lid and continue to cook for another 5 minutes, until nearly all the liquid has evaporated.

Turn off the heat and add the mint leaves, the juice of 1 lemon and ¼ teaspoon of black pepper. Mix well and leave to sit with the lid off so that some excess water can evaporate.

For the vegan feta, put the drained cashews into a food processor with the tofu, garlic powder, nutritional yeast, the rest of the lemon juice, 4 tablespoons of olive oil and 1 teaspoon of salt. Blend until it all comes together. Add to the leek and spinach mixture and mix well.

Spread the mixture evenly in an ovenproof dish (approx. 32 x 22cm). Lay the first sheet of filo pastry on top, trimming the pastry to fit your dish if necessary, using scissors. Brush the filo with olive oil, using a pastry brush. Repeat with the other 6 sheets.

Bake in the oven for 25 minutes, until the filo pastry topping starts to turn golden. The easiest way to cut this is using a sharp knife or scissors – then serve and enjoy!

LEEKS

Mexican Leek and Cheese Toastie

I remember the first time I tried creamed leek. I couldn't believe the flavour. Growing up in Ireland, everyone loves a cheese toastie – the simple combination of cheese, mustard and onion is a classic. This is our take on the classic cheese toastie, transformed into tasty quesadillas. We have switched out the onion for creamy leeks and kept the classic cheese, mustard and pickles.

9 INGREDIENTS

1. 1 x 400ml tin of full-fat coconut milk
2. 300g leeks
3. 150g roasted red peppers, from a jar
4. 1 avocado
5. 50g gherkins or cornichons (optional)
6. 100g vegan Cheddar cheese
7. juice of ½ a lemon
8. 4 large wholewheat or corn tortilla wraps
9. 4 tsp Dijon mustard

Place the tin of coconut milk in the fridge or freezer while you prepare the rest of the ingredients.

Finely slice the leeks, including the green parts, into rounds and give them a good wash. Drain the peppers from their brine and slice them into strips. Cut the avocado in half and remove the stone, then scoop out the flesh and slice it into long strips. Slice the gherkins into thin strips. Grate the vegan Cheddar.

Heat a large non-stick frying pan on a high heat. Once hot, add 1 tablespoon of olive oil, the sliced leeks and a pinch of salt. Cook for 5 minutes, stirring occasionally.

Take the tin of coconut milk from the fridge and remove the cream from the top, but none of the water. Add this coconut cream to the leeks, along with the lemon juice, and mix through. Cook for a further 5 minutes, stirring occasionally. (Keep the coconut water to use in a smoothie or as a stock for another dish – it will store for a week in the fridge.)

Taste the creamed leeks and season to your liking. Remove from the pan and give the pan a quick clean and wipe dry.

Put the pan back on a medium heat and add a tortilla. Heat up for 30 seconds. On one half of the tortilla spread 1 teaspoon of mustard, add a good dollop of the creamed leeks (approx. a quarter), a few slices of red pepper, a few slices of gherkin, a few slices of avocado and sprinkle with a quarter of the vegan cheese. Fold in half and allow to cook for another minute. Carefully flip the tortilla over and cook for a further minute, until it starts to crisp up and the cheese starts to melt.

Remove from the heat and slice into quarters. Repeat with the rest of the tortillas and filling.

LEEKS

Lentil, Coconut and Leek Baked Curry

This is a lovely simple baked curry, where the oven does all the hard work for you. It's hearty, nourishing and super-delicious. The baked leek on top gives it a lovely texture. Serve with toasted wholemeal pitta breads for a delicious dinner!

10 INGREDIENTS

1. ½ a thumb-size piece of fresh ginger (12g)

2. 1 x 400ml tin of coconut milk

3. 2 tbsp curry powder

4. 1 tsp ground cumin

5. juice of 1 lime

6. 3 tbsp tamari or soy sauce

7. 2 x 400g tins of cooked lentils

8. 500g sweet potatoes

9. 15g fresh coriander, basil or chives

10. 2 medium leeks

Preheat the oven to 200°C fan/220°C/gas 7.

To make the sauce, peel and roughly chop the ginger and put it into a blender with the coconut milk, curry powder, ground cumin, lime juice, 2 tablespoons of tamari, 400ml of water, 1 teaspoon of salt and ¼ teaspoon of black pepper. Blend until smooth.

Drain and rinse the lentils. Chop the sweet potatoes into bite-size pieces. Put the sweet potatoes and lentils into a large deep oven dish (we use a 32 x 22cm dish), then add the sauce and mix well.

Roughly chop the herbs and set aside. Cut the whole leeks crossways into 8cm pieces, give them a good wash, then cut them in half lengthways. Put the leeks into a bowl and mix with 2 tablespoons of olive oil and 1 tablespoon of tamari. Place the sliced long leeks on a separate lined baking tray with the cut side (the centre of the leek) facing down.

Put the casserole dish and the tray into the oven and bake for 25 minutes, or until the sweet potatoes are soft and cooked through and the leeks are nicely roasted and just starting to char.

Remove from the oven. Place the roasted leeks on top of the curry, with the cut side facing up. Garnish with the chopped fresh herbs and serve.

LEEKS

Easy Sausage, White Bean and Leek Baked Casserole

A delicious hearty mid-week dinner, with a perfect balance of comfort and nourishment between the vegan sausages, beans and veg. The leeks become soft and succulent when cooked in a casserole like this.

10 INGREDIENTS

1. 6 vegan sausages

2. 2 large leeks

3. 2 cloves of garlic

4. 1 medium red chilli

5. 1 large carrot

6. 2 x 400g tins of butter beans

7. 100g vegan Cheddar cheese

8. 1 x 400g tin of chopped tomatoes

9. 250ml veg stock

10. 80g fresh breadcrumbs

Defrost the sausages, if using frozen. Preheat the oven to 180°C fan/ 200°C/ gas 6.

Cut the leeks into large slices about 3cm long, including the green parts, and give them a good wash. Cut the vegan sausages into bite-size pieces. Peel and finely slice the garlic. Finely slice the chilli, omitting the seeds if you don't like it too hot. Chop the carrot into small rounds. Drain and rinse the butter beans. Grate the vegan Cheddar.

Heat 1 tablespoon of olive oil in a large wide-bottomed ovenproof frying pan on a high heat. Once hot, add the sausages and cook for 2 minutes. Add the leeks, carrot and a good pinch of salt and cook for 3 minutes, stirring regularly. Add the garlic and chilli and cook for a further minute, then lower the heat to medium, put a lid on the pan and leave the veg to steam for about 8–10 minutes, stirring occasionally. If the veg start sticking to the bottom of the pan, add 1–2 tablespoons of veg stock.

Add the chopped tomatoes, veg stock and butter beans and mix well. Bring to the boil, then reduce to a simmer for 2 minutes. Add 1½ teaspoons of salt and ½ teaspoon of black pepper and mix well. Add half the grated vegan Cheddar and stir. Taste and add more salt and pepper if it needs it.

Put the rest of the vegan cheese into a bowl. Add the breadcrumbs, along with a pinch of black pepper and ½ tablespoon of oil, and mix well. Sprinkle the breadcrumb topping evenly over the veg in the pan, then transfer to the oven and cook for 15 minutes, or until the breadcrumbs are golden brown.

Remove carefully from the oven and serve.

№ 9

MUSHROOMS

We are serious fans of mushrooms and could have written a book of just mushroom recipes. In this section we wanted to show their versatility and how wonderful they can be!

We have made some beautiful mushroom sausages with sun-dried tomatoes (page 229), we make some vegan 'scallops' on miso pumpkin purée (page 241), for an epic special-occasion meal, the mushroom kofta curry (page 244) is a simple crowd-pleaser, and the mushroom and caramelized onion sausage rolls (page 233) are one of Steve's kids' favourite meals!

Mushrooms are fungi, of which there are millions of varieties. It is believed that there are more fungus varieties than plant varieties. Mushrooms are incredible, in that they have a mycelium network formed by their roots, through which they can communicate and transfer nutrients between each other.

The two most common mushrooms – button and flat cap – are the same variety, just at different stages of growth. Button is the younger of the two, with hardly any stem and very mild in flavour, whereas flat cap are grown-up button mushrooms with more flavour. The next two most common mushrooms – Portobello and chestnut mushrooms – tend to have more flavour and are also the same variety at different stages of growth, with chestnut being the young Portobello. Oyster mushrooms get their name from their colour and not their flavour, and grow on dead tree stumps in the wild. They contain a lot of moisture, so they reduce down once cooked. They are also available in pink or yellow, which both look cool! Shiitake was originally a Chinese mushroom that is now cultivated all over the world. It is heralded for its health properties, and has a meaty, substantial texture and flavour.

There is a wealth of mushrooms that are starting to be more commonly available – at times we have sold lion's mane, miitake, enoki, beech, black trumpet and chanterelle in the shop, and we adore learning and cooking with these different varieties.

BUYING & STORING

Choose firm mushrooms that are not too spongy, and where relevant and possible turn the mushrooms upside down and have a look at their gills, which should be dry and firm. Avoid any mushrooms that are wet or soggy or woody. In terms of storing, it is best to remove the mushrooms from any plastic packets, if this is how you bought them, as this can cause condensation and make them go soggy. Store them in the fridge in a paper bag. Some people put their mushrooms in the sun to absorb more vitamin D; however, if left too long in the sun they will dry out and become woody. Alternatively you can spend 20 minutes outside in direct sunlight and you will generally get all your vitamin D requirements for the day.

Mushrooms can be foraged, and it is something that we love to do. We remember having such fun with our friend Nick in Devon, hunting for turkey tail and chicken of the woods mushrooms, but you should only do this with someone who is qualified and knows the different varieties, as there can be many poisonous mushrooms.

GROWING

Commercially produced mushrooms are grown in controlled chambers that manage the humidity and temperature, air flow and light and can be grown all year round.

Wild mushrooms all have their own season, and generally it starts just after the summer, once the temperature drops slightly and it becomes damper, and finishes before the first frost. Different mushrooms will grow better on different growing mediums – shiitake prefer wood bark while button mushrooms are generally grown in compost. We have experimented with growing mushrooms many times, up in storerooms in big tubs or in cupboards in containers, and have always got such pleasure when it works! It's great fun to buy a kit and try to grow them at home.

COOKING

The big mushroom debate is about cleaning them. Some chefs never wet mushrooms, as they believe they become soggy and lose some of their absorbent properties, while others recommend brushing or cleaning them with a dry cloth. If you are going to wash your mushrooms in water, don't soak them. Instead, think of dunking them like you would a biscuit in a cup of tea, or wipe them with a damp cloth.

Mushrooms are versatile, meaty and absorb flavours wonderfully. Shallow-fry them and add them to a creamy pasta dish, as we have done in the easy creamy mushroom pasta (page 234), and marinate or cook them with deep umami flavours such as tamari or soy sauce, as we have done in the spiced Chinese mushroom noodles (page 235). They are also great baked, as in the rich and creamy mushroom Wellington (page 243), and grilled or fried with garlic on some fresh toast, like we did in the easy garlic mushrooms on chilli smashed avocado (page 230).

NUTRITION

Mushrooms are a good source of essential B vitamins and other immune-supporting nutrients such as selenium. White button mushrooms can be one of the few plant-food sources of vitamin D, which is important for calcium absorption, immune function, heart health and protecting bone health. They have also been linked to helping improve cardiovascular function, and even help protect against cancer.

80g of mushrooms, 14 baby button mushrooms, 4 large closed cup mushrooms or 1 large flat mushroom are considered to be one of your 5-a-day.

Cheesy Mushroom and Sun-dried Tomato Sausages on Toast

Claire, a wonderful chef who worked with us, used to make a variation of these in the café about ten years ago. The staff always devoured them, and often they didn't even make it out to the customers! Here we use quinoa as a base and layer on taste to give a full-flavoured sausage. We like to serve these with vegan mayo and some sourdough bread.

10 INGREDIENTS
1. 65g cashew nuts
2. 1 x 400g tin of butter beans
3. 75g vegan Cheddar cheese
4. 1 medium onion
5. 200g button mushrooms
6. 50g sun-dried tomatoes
7. 120g cooked quinoa or brown rice
8. ¼ tsp chilli powder
9. 10 tbsp plain white flour
10. 25g sesame seeds, for rolling

Chop the cashews into small pieces. Drain and rinse the butter beans. Grate the vegan cheese. Peel and dice the onion. Slice the mushrooms into thin bite-size pieces. Soak the sun-dried tomatoes in boiling water for 5 minutes, then cut into small strips.

Put a large non-stick pan on a high heat. Once hot, add 1 tablespoon of olive oil, then add the onion, mushrooms and 1 teaspoon of salt. Reduce the heat to medium and fry for 6–7 minutes, stirring regularly, until the mushrooms decrease in volume by almost half and the onions start to brown.

Put all the ingredients except the flour and sesame seeds into a large bowl and add ½ teaspoon of salt and ½ teaspoon of black pepper and mash the whole mixture until everything is nicely broken down. Alternatively, use a food processor and blend until you get a smooth texture.

Stir through the flour – the mixture should hold its shape. Split the mixture into approx. 75g portions and roll them into 12cm-long sausage shapes. Roll them in sesame seeds so that you get a nice crispy crust.

Heat a non-stick frying pan on a medium heat. Once hot, add 1 tablespoon of oil and the sausages – they should all have enough room to touch the bottom and brown on each side, so cook them in batches if your pan is small. Fry until brown on all sides.

Serve with your favourite toast and some vegan mayo for a lovely breakfast treat!

MUSHROOMS

Easy Garlic Mushrooms on Chilli Smashed Avocado

A lovely easy weekend brunch or a meal that works at any time of the day. We like to use sourdough bread, but use whatever bread you prefer. This is simple good food that nourishes the soul!

8 INGREDIENTS

1. 250g button mushrooms
2. 1 small red chilli
3. 2 cloves of garlic
4. 1 tbsp tamari or soy sauce
5. 150g baby spinach
6. 2 limes
7. 4 slices of bread
8. 2 ripe avocados

Finely slice the mushrooms and the chilli (leaving the seeds in if you like it hot). Peel and finely chop the garlic.

Put a non-stick pan on a high heat, then add 1 tablespoon of olive oil and leave to heat up. Once hot, add the mushrooms and cook for 4 minutes, stirring regularly. Add the garlic and cook for a further minute. Add the tamari and stir well so that all the mushrooms and garlic get a coating. Mix in the spinach and turn off the heat – the spinach should wilt down in the residual heat. Squeeze in the juice of 1 lime and mix it through.

Toast the bread. Cut the avocados in half, remove the stones, spoon out the flesh and slice it small. Put it into a bowl with the juice of the second lime, ½ teaspoon of salt, a good pinch of black pepper and half the sliced chilli. Mash it with a fork until it reaches your desired texture.

Spoon the avocado on to the toasted bread, dividing it evenly. If you want to really splash out, you can drizzle a little olive oil (1 tablespoon per 2 slices) on the toasted bread first. Top with the garlic mushrooms and garnish with the rest of the chilli.

MAKES 4 sausage rolls   **TAKES** 30 minutes

Mushroom and Caramelized Onion Sausage Rolls

All Steve's kids adore these, and they don't even know they're eating mushrooms! These rolls are so good – sweet, earthy, crispy and chewy, definitely one of the nicest sausage rolls we've tasted!

10 INGREDIENTS
1. 1 x 320g sheet of vegan puff pastry
2. 250g oyster mushrooms or mushrooms of choice
3. 2 cloves of garlic, or ½ tsp garlic powder
4. 1 medium red onion
5. 2 tbsp tamari or soy sauce
6. 3 tbsp maple syrup
7. 3 tbsp balsamic vinegar
8. 100g cashew nuts
9. 50ml oat milk or non-dairy milk of choice
10. 2 tbsp sesame seeds

If using frozen puff pastry, make sure it is fully thawed. Preheat the oven to 200°C fan/220°C/gas 7. Line a baking tray with baking parchment.

Slice the oyster mushrooms. Peel and finely chop the garlic. Peel and finely slice the red onion. Heat 1 tablespoon of olive oil in a medium frying pan over a high heat. Once hot, add the mushrooms and a pinch of salt and cook for 3–5 minutes, until all the moisture from the mushrooms begins to evaporate and they begin to brown. Reduce the heat and add the garlic and a pinch of black pepper. Cook for 1 minute, stirring so that the garlic doesn't burn. Add the tamari, stirring to coat all the mushrooms, then remove from the heat. Transfer the mushrooms to a bowl, then carefully wipe out the pan and use it for the caramelized onions.

Heat 1 tablespoon of olive oil in the pan over a high heat. Once hot, add the sliced red onion and a pinch of salt and black pepper. Cook on a medium heat for 5 minutes, stirring occasionally, until the onions are browned and softened. Add the maple syrup and stir to coat the onions, then reduce to a low heat and cook for 2–3 minutes, until the onions are sticky. Add the vinegar and cook for another 5 minutes, until all the liquid has been absorbed. Remove from the heat and set aside.

Put the cashews into a food processor and pulse until they have a breadcrumb consistency. Add the caramelized onions, mushrooms and ½ teaspoon of black pepper. Blend until the mixture comes together but is not too smooth. Taste and add more salt and pepper, if it needs it. Remove from the processor and divide into 4 x 80g sausages, approx. 12–13 cm long.

Roll out the puff pastry on a lightly floured surface and cut into 4 even rectangles approx. 12 x 16cm. Place a sausage at one side of one of the pastry rectangles, 2–3cm in from the edge. Roll up the sausage in the pastry until the pastry overlaps. Brush with oat milk to seal. Place the sausage roll seam side down on your work surface and gently press down on the roll with the palm of your hand. Repeat with the remaining sausages and pastry.

Using a pastry brush, brush each sausage roll with a light coating of oat milk and sprinkle with the sesame seeds. Place them on the lined baking tray and cook in the oven for 20 minutes, or until the pastry is golden brown.

MUSHROOMS

SERVES 2–3   TAKES 20 minutes

Easy Creamy Mushroom Pasta

This recipe is the perfect example of flavour synergy, where the sum of the parts is greater than when separate. It seems very simple, but the result is a fabulous creamy pasta dish that is a family favourite. It makes a perfect bowl of comforting goodness.

8 INGREDIENTS

1. 100g cashew nuts
2. 250g wholemeal pasta (we normally use penne)
3. 1 large red onion
4. 250g mushrooms of choice (we like oyster/ shiitake/ chestnut)
5. 1½ tsp garlic powder
6. 2 tbsp tamari or soy sauce
7. 500ml non-dairy milk of choice
8. juice of ½ a lemon

In a bowl, cover the cashew nuts with boiling water and leave to soak for 10 minutes.

Bring a large saucepan of water to the boil and add 1 tablespoon of salt (don't worry, most of this will go down the drain but it will help season your pasta from within). Put your pasta on to boil and cook according to the packet instructions.

Peel and dice the onion and finely chop the mushrooms. Heat a large non-stick pan over a high heat. Once hot, add 1 tablespoon of olive oil, along with the onions and ½ teaspoon of salt. Reduce the heat to medium and cook for 4–5 minutes to brown them slightly, stirring occasionally.

Add the chopped mushrooms and ½ teaspoon of garlic powder and cook for 3–5 minutes. Add the tamari and cook for a minute. Remove the mushrooms to a plate and set aside.

While the mushrooms are cooking, make the cashew sauce. Drain and rinse the cashew nuts and put them into a high-speed blender/food processor with the non-dairy milk, lemon juice, 1 teaspoon of garlic powder, ½ teaspoon of salt and ¼ teaspoon of ground black pepper. Blend on high speed until very smooth.*

Add the creamy cashew sauce to the pan you cooked the mushrooms in and reduce the heat to low. Cook for 1–2 minutes, stirring continuously, to allow the sauce to thicken.

Drain the pasta when cooked, keeping some of the cooking water. Mix the pasta with the cashew sauce, coating the pasta well – if the sauce is too thick, add a little pasta water until you get your desired creamy texture. Add the mushrooms, then taste and add more salt and black pepper, if needed.

Garnish with a fresh chilli, seeds removed and sliced finely. Or the leaves from 3 sprigs of fresh oregano or thyme, sprinkled over the top.

*If your blender or food processor has not blended until super-smooth, and there are some little nut pieces left, pour the sauce through a sieve into a pan, add 2 tablespoons of sieved cornflour, and allow to reduce and thicken on a high heat for 2–3 minutes, stirring continuously.

Spiced Chinese Mushroom Noodles

Inspired by the dan dan noodle dish from Sichuan province, known for its famous pepper and traditionally spicy dishes, this is super-tasty and a real crowd-pleaser. Use wholemeal noodles to add more fibre. If you have Sichuan pepper it adds a nice authentic feel to this dish, but if you don't have any you can just use black pepper.

10 INGREDIENTS

1. 200g mushrooms

2. 4 cloves of garlic

3. 250g dried noodles

4. 1 pack of tenderstem broccoli

5. 4 tbsp tamari or soy sauce

6. 1 tbsp chilli flakes

7. 1 tbsp sesame seeds, plus extra to serve

8. 2 tbsp coconut or brown sugar

9. 2 tsp rice wine vinegar/any white vinegar

10. 1½ tbsp tahini or nut butter of choice

Finely chop the mushrooms. Peel and finely chop the garlic. Cook the noodles according to the packet instructions. Add the broccoli to the noodle water for the last 4 minutes of the noodle cooking time. Drain and rinse the noodles and broccoli under cold water to stop them cooking, then separate them, reserving some cooking liquid to thin the sauce later on.

Put the rest of the ingredients into a bowl, along with 2 tablespoons of olive oil and 1½ teaspoons of black pepper. Mix until nice and smooth.

Heat a wide-bottomed non-stick pan on a high heat for 2 minutes, then add 1 teaspoon of oil and the mushrooms. Cook for 2–3 minutes, until the mushrooms release their liquid. Add 4 tablespoons of the sauce and mix well, so that the mushrooms soak the sauce up and are nicely charred. Remove the mushrooms from the pan and set aside.

Heat the pan over a high heat. Once hot, add the broccoli and reduce the heat to medium. We are aiming to get a nice char on the broccoli – cook for 2–3 minutes on each side, then remove from the pan and roughly chop each stem into thirds.

Add 5–6 tablespoons of noodle water and the remaining sauce to the pan. Add the noodles and heat through for 2 minutes, stirring regularly.

Transfer to serving bowls, and top with the mushrooms and broccoli. Sprinkle with extra sesame seeds and enjoy!

MUSHROOMS

Creamy Mushroom Puff Pastry Pie

A lovely hearty family dinner that is stuffed with melt-in-your-mouth veg, all topped with a crispy pastry topping! The first time we tried this, Dave had been busy doing some DIY in his house with a friend, Marcin, and they ate the whole thing between them – it was just so tasty!

10 INGREDIENTS

1. 1 x 320g sheet of vegan ready-rolled puff pastry

2. 400g mushrooms

3. 1 medium leek

4. 3 cloves of garlic

5. 200g sweet potatoes

6. 200g potatoes

7. 1 tbsp Dijon mustard

8. 8 tbsp plain flour

9. 800ml oat milk or non-dairy milk of choice, plus extra for brushing

10. 1 tsp garlic powder

If using frozen puff pastry, take it out of the freezer to defrost and reach room temperature.

Preheat the oven to 200°C fan/220°C/gas 7.

Cut the mushrooms into thick slices. Slice the leek into 1cm rounds, including the green parts, and give them a good wash. Peel and finely chop the garlic. Leaving the skins on, cut both lots of potatoes into 1cm pieces.

Put 1 tablespoon of oil in a wide-bottomed non-stick pan on a high heat. Once hot, add the mushrooms and fry for 4–5 minutes until they start to colour, then add the garlic and fry for another couple of minutes. Remove from the pan and set aside.

Using the same pan, add the sweet potatoes, potatoes, leek and 1 teaspoon of salt. Mix well and cook for 5 minutes, stirring regularly. Reduce the heat to low–medium, put a lid on the pan, and leave the veg to steam in their own juices for another 10 minutes, or until the potatoes and sweet potatoes are cooked through. Turn off the heat and put the cooked mushrooms back into the pan along with the mustard.

To make the béchamel sauce, put 8 tablespoons of olive oil into a pan on a medium heat. Once hot, sieve in the flour and cook for 1–2 minutes, stirring continuously with a whisk until it goes slightly golden. Slowly add the oat milk, stirring continuously. Bring to the boil, then reduce to a gentle simmer, stirring to be careful that nothing sticks to the bottom. Add 2 teaspoons of salt, ¼ teaspoon of ground black pepper and the garlic powder. Once simmering, and when it reaches a creamy texture, remove from the heat. Taste and adjust the seasoning if it needs it.

Add the sauce to the mushroom mixture, then transfer to a casserole or pie dish (we use a 20 x 30cm pie dish) and leave to cool for 10 minutes.

Roll out the pastry on a lightly floured surface and cut it to fit the top of the pie dish. Gently score the top in a criss-cross pattern and lift it on to the pie dish. Crimp the edges of the pastry around the top of the dish using your fingers or a fork. Brush the top of the pastry with a little extra oat milk to help it turn golden.

Cook in the oven for 25 minutes, until the pastry is golden and crisp. This goes wonderfully on its own, or you could serve it with a green salad or in winter with roasted potatoes.

'Scallops' on Miso Pumpkin Purée

This makes a wonderful celebration dinner. It is very sensual, impressive and surprisingly easy to make.

9 INGREDIENTS

1. 2 cloves of garlic

2. 4 king oyster mushrooms or 12–14 large button mushrooms

3. 3 sheets of nori seaweed

4. 1 litre veg stock, plus 60ml for the pumpkin purée

5. 3 tbsp tamari or soy sauce

6. 200g pumpkin purée or cooked pumpkin

7. 1 tbsp miso

8. 3 tbsp white wine

9. 1 tbsp maple syrup

Peel and finely chop the garlic. Cut the stems of the king oyster mushrooms into even 2–3cm rounds like thick coins or medallions and carefully score in a criss-cross design on the top and bottom of each mushroom to help them cook fully, being sure not to cut so deep that they fall apart. Be sure to keep the caps of the mushrooms for use in any of the other mushroom recipes in this chapter. If using button mushrooms, trim the stalk and make a thin slice from the top of the mushroom so it resembles a flat scallop medallion. Carefully score in a criss-cross design on the top and bottom of each mushroom as mentioned above.

Tear the nori sheets and put them into a pan with the mushrooms, 1 litre of veg stock, 3 tablespoons of tamari and the garlic. Simmer for 15 minutes for the king oyster mushrooms or 10 minutes for the button mushrooms, until the mushrooms are mostly cooked but still firm. Remove the mushrooms from the pan and dry on a clean tea towel or kitchen paper. (You can save the stock and use it to make a quick miso soup base.)

Put the pumpkin purée into a blender along with the miso, 60ml of veg stock, 4 tablespoons of olive oil and ½ teaspoon of salt. Blend until smooth and creamy.

Heat a wide non-stick pan over a high heat. Once hot, add 2 tablespoons of olive oil, then carefully add the 'scallops' and reduce the heat to medium. Turn the mushrooms so they sear and brown on both sides for 2–3 minutes.

Carefully add the wine (it will sizzle a little) and let it reduce, then add the maple syrup and stir around the pan. Continue to turn the scallops until they are a lovely golden brown on both sides. Once cooked, remove from the pan.

To serve, put a generous tablespoon of pumpkin purée on each plate, then, using the back of a spoon, press down in the centre and move it quickly to the side to create a swoosh or a lovely shape on which to place the 'scallops'. Divide the mushroom 'scallops' between the plates, and prepare for family and friends to be suitably impressed.

MUSHROOMS

High Protein Mushroom Burger

These burgers are delicious and very easy to make. We like to serve them with chips and your favourite burger toppings, such as chilli ketchup, mayo, sliced tomato, lettuce or gherkin. In this recipe we use a neutral-tasting protein powder to absorb the moisture and bind the burgers – it's not essential, and you can use ground flax seed instead, which works similarly. We love to use oyster mushrooms, but you can use any type of mushroom.

10 INGREDIENTS

1. 250g mushrooms of choice

2. 1 medium onion

3. 2 cloves of garlic

4. 1 x 400g tin of black beans

5. 1 small red chilli, or a pinch of chilli powder

6. 3 tbsp tamari or soy sauce

7. 100g oat flakes

8. 2 tbsp protein powder or ground flax seed

9. 2 tbsp nutritional yeast

10. 2 tbsp peanut or almond butter

Finely chop the mushrooms. Peel and finely chop the onion and garlic. Drain and rinse the black beans. Finely chop the red chilli.

Heat 1 tablespoon of olive oil in a large non-stick pan on a high heat. Once hot, add the mushrooms and onion and cook for 3–4 minutes, stirring regularly. Reduce the heat to medium and add the chopped garlic. Cook for another minute. Add the tamari and cook for a further minute, stirring so that all the mix gets an even coating of tamari.

Put the oat flakes into a food processor and pulse them a few times to a coarse flour-like consistency.

Put the rinsed beans into a large bowl and mash, using a potato masher. Add the pulsed oat flakes, mushroom mixture, protein powder or ground flax seed, nutritional yeast, nut butter, ½ teaspoon of black pepper and the chilli to the bowl. Mix well, using a spoon or clean hands. Taste the mixture and add seasoning if needed. Alternatively, if you like a smooth texture, you can put all the above ingredients into a food processor and pulse until you reach your desired texture.

Shape the mixture into 6 burgers. Put the pan back on a high heat and coat with 1 tablespoon of oil. Once hot, add the burgers and cook them on each side for 3 minutes, until they start to char and brown. You can also bake the burgers in the oven at 180°C fan/200°C/gas 6 for 15 minutes, or until cooked through, turning them once.

Serve in a burger bun of your choice, with barbecue sauce (page 276), vegan mayo (page 275) and some lettuce and sliced tomatoes.

Rich and Creamy Mushroom Wellington

Our friends had a restaurant called the 3Qs and they used to serve this super-rich and incredible tasty mushroom Wellington. This recipe is an easier-to-make version that is still a real treat! Goes great served with the wine and thyme gravy on page 270. It makes a lovely centrepiece for a Sunday dinner or a celebration.

10 INGREDIENTS

1. 1 large red onion

2. 3 cloves of garlic

3. 1 x 400g tin of chickpeas

4. 10g fresh thyme

5. 300g mushrooms of choice

6. 170g cashew nuts

7. 75ml white wine

8. 1 x 160ml tin of coconut cream or 1 x 400ml tin of coconut milk

9. 70g fresh breadcrumbs

10. 1 x 320g sheet of vegan puff pastry

Preheat oven to 180°C fan/200°C/gas 6. Line a baking tray with baking parchment.

Peel and finely chop the red onion and garlic. Drain and rinse the chickpeas. Pick the thyme leaves. Finely chop half the mushrooms and use a food processor to pulse the remaining mushrooms and drained chickpeas until they become small but still have some texture. If you don't have a food processor, just chop them all up finely.

Roughly chop the cashews. Spread them on a baking tray with a pinch of salt. Bake for 6 minutes until golden brown, then remove and set aside.

Heat 2 tablespoons of olive oil in a large non-stick pan over a high heat. Once hot, add the onion and cook for 5 minutes, stirring occasionally. Add the mushroom mixture and the garlic and continue to cook for 4–5 minutes. Once the mushrooms start to reduce in size, add the white wine and leave it to evaporate for 1–2 minutes, then add 1 teaspoon of salt and the thyme leaves. Stir to coat the mushrooms and cook for a further 3 minutes. Remove from the heat. Add the coconut cream, or if using coconut milk, just add the top layer of cream from the tin and stir through.

Mix through the cashew nuts, breadcrumbs, ¾ teaspoon of salt and ½ teaspoon of ground black pepper. Taste and adjust the seasoning to your liking. Allow to cool for 15 minutes in the fridge.

On a lightly floured surface, roll out the pastry to 30 x 40cm, and transfer to the lined baking tray. Add your mixture along the centre of the sheet of pastry in a rounded Swiss roll shape, leaving about 8–10cm at each end and enough pastry on either side to be able to cover the filling. Wrap the filling tightly with the pastry, sealing at both ends like a parcel, and flip over so the seam is facing down. Gently score the top in diagonal lines to create a pattern while baking, then brush with a little non-dairy milk of your choice. Bake in the oven for 25 minutes, or until golden and cooked through.

While the Wellington is baking, make the gravy on page 270 and prepare any veg to serve with this. We often serve it with mashed potato, broccoli and roasted carrots.

Once cooked, garnish with a few sprigs of fresh thyme and enjoy.

MUSHROOMS

Mushroom Kofta Curry

While you might be more familiar with meatballs, Indian-style koftas – which means balls – are traditionally made with paneer and vegetables, so we've created these to add texture and bite to this sweet creamy dish. Serve with pickled red onions, fresh coriander and naan bread or flatbreads for a wonderful meal.

10 INGREDIENTS

1. 200g firm tofu

2. 2 red onions

3. 4 cloves of garlic

4. ½ thumb-size piece of fresh ginger

5. 150g roasted red peppers, from a jar

6. 20g fresh coriander, plus extra to garnish

7. 400g mushrooms

8. 4 tbsp tamari or soy sauce

9. 1 x 400ml tin of full-fat coconut milk

10. 2 tbsp curry powder

Preheat the oven to 200°C fan/220°C/gas 7. Line a baking tray with baking parchment.

Cut the tofu into 1cm cubes. Peel and finely chop the red onions. Peel and finely chop the garlic and ginger. Slice the red peppers into strips. Finely chop the coriander. Cut the mushrooms into bite-size pieces.

Heat a large non-stick frying pan on high heat. Once hot, add 1 tablespoon of oil along with the tofu and fry for 5–6 minutes, then remove and set aside. Place the pan back on a high heat with another tablespoon of oil and add the onions, mushrooms, garlic, ginger and coriander. Cook for 5–6 minutes, stirring regularly, then add the tamari and a pinch of black pepper. Cook for another minute or so, ensuring you mix the tamari through, then remove from the heat.

Put half the mushroom mixture into a blender with the cooked tofu and blend until smooth. Remove and shape into 15 small golfball-size balls and place on the lined baking tray. Using a pastry brush, gently brush the balls with plenty of olive oil. Bake for 15 minutes.

Clean out the food processor and put in the coconut milk, roasted red pepper and curry powder. Blend until smooth to make a sauce – it should have a lovely vibrant colour. Pour the sauce into the frying pan and add the reserved mushroom and onion mix. Heat on a medium heat for 2–3 minutes. Taste and add more salt and pepper if it needs it.

Remove the koftas from the oven and add to the curry, garnished with the coriander leaves.

Serve with pickled onions (page 57) and toasted wholemeal pitta breads.

POTATOES

Can you imagine where we would be without the potato? Who doesn't love a chip, with its perfect crispy outside and soft, sweet, delicious inside? Or its close cousin, the roast potato?

Potatoes are linked to so many of our favourite dishes, and are part of many of our childhood memories. In Ireland, we call them 'spuds', after the name for the three-pronged fork used to dig potatoes here.

The potato is a tuber (a swollen root) that is part of the nightshade family, along with tomatoes. It is the third-biggest food crop globally, after rice and corn. A field of potatoes throws up more food per acre than any other food crop in Europe. They grow well in all but harsh environments.

Nowadays, in many supermarkets, potatoes have been reduced to generic 'red' or 'white', but there are massive differences in varieties and uses. When we first started The Happy Pear as a greengrocer shop, customers used to buy a 10kg bag of potatoes for the week and we would sell a huge variety, as people would seek out different things from different potatoes, for example, Maris Pipers for chips or dry fluffy potatoes like Golden Wonder for roasties. The first early potatoes in early April used to cause quite a stir, and go for a decent price too.

In nature an ecosystem is generally healthier when there is more diversity, and it's similar within our food systems, and in this case with potatoes the more varieties we cultivate and grow, the more resilient and the more diverse we will be. If you can find older varieties, you will be amazed at how different potatoes can be. Recently a friend, Simon, shared with us an old variety he was growing called a Pink Fir Apple, which looked amazing, a little tuber with lots of knuckles and vibrant pink spots – it was beautiful and, wow, so incredibly tasty.

You will often see the word 'waxy' and 'floury' on bags of potatoes. New potatoes are waxy, meaning they are high in water and don't absorb much liquid; they don't disintegrate and are very well suited for boiling, as they hold their shape. 'Floury' kinds, such as Maris Piper, are fluffy with a low water content and are better suited for baking, roasting, mash and chips.

BUYING & STORING

If you buy potatoes from the supermarket in a plastic bag, take them out as soon as you get home, as condensation will build and they will start to rot. Dirty potatoes last best – the dirt acts as a protective layer against sunlight and drying out.

New potatoes have very thin skins and only last days, whereas maincrop thick-skinned potatoes can last months in the fridge or in a cool dark cupboard. By winter, potatoes will start to sprout in anticipation of spring, provided they haven't turned green – simply knock off the chits and they are fine to eat. If your potatoes turn green, which is a sign of the toxin solanine, you should discard them. This often happens from storing them in too much sunlight.

Potatoes are best stored in the cold and the dark, and if you buy dirty potatoes, they last fine out of the fridge until mid-winter.

NUTRITION

The skin of a potato and the part just below the skin is the most nutritious, containing lots of minerals and most of the fibre, so it is best to keep the skin on your potatoes. They have almost all the nutrients we need, and this is why potatoes became very popular among poorer people, certainly in Ireland, and other parts of the world. Potatoes are a rich source of potassium, which is good for your blood, bones and muscles and helps with digestion. They are also rich in starch, like bananas, pasta and bread, so provide an easy energy source. Unfortunately it is because of this high starch content that potatoes are not considered part of your 5-a-day.

GROWING

Potatoes are in season all year round. Waxy thin-skinned new potatoes are available in spring, followed by the main crop of potatoes which is picked around June and lasts for the full year, to the following June. When a potato is left in a cupboard for too long it will start to sprout or grow shoots. This is known as chitting.

Potatoes are super-easy to grow and can be grown in tyres or vertical set-ups to fit even balconies or smaller spaces. One planted sprouted potato will produce many potatoes when harvested. In spring, plant sprouted potatoes 30cm apart and cover them with soil. When the shoots reach 20cm tall, mound up soil around the base of the shoots, covering the stems halfway – this is known as earthing up. Harvest in autumn, when the plants start to wilt and die, as this is a sure sign that the potatoes have finished growing.

COOKING

Potatoes are quite possibly the most versatile vegetable that exists – they are great baked, boiled, roasted, fried, and let's not forget the beloved mash! In this chapter we wanted to show some of our favourites, from the crowd-pleasing creamy leek and potato pies (page 255) to the Mexican-inspired potato rösti stack (page 252), to curries like the spinach, potato and coconut curry (page 267) and the super-indulgent creamy dauphinoise potatoes (page 256).

We use them as toppings for some epic pies, such as the chickpea, potato and pesto bake (page 260) and the comforting, easy cottage pie (page 264). But with these recipes we wanted to show how good potatoes can be when they are the star of the show, for example, our Goan-style spiced jackfruit and potato 'chops' (page 263), the creamy potato and kale croquettes with umami mayo (page 259), or even possibly our favourite way to cook potatoes, the spicy smashed potatoes with sriracha mayo (page 254). We hope by the end of this chapter you can see them as so much more than just mash and chips.

Potato Hash Browns and Vegan Sausages with Pan-fried Mushrooms

A super-tasty weekend brekkie that is really worth the extra effort. There is a great variety of tastes and textures and it works well as a brunch. We love to serve this with hot toast and vegan mayo or pesto (page 275) for a delicious start to the day!

8 INGREDIENTS

1. 700g potatoes
2. 4 spring onions
3. 2 cloves of garlic
4. 4 vegan sausages
5. 400g mushrooms
6. 20 cherry tomatoes (multi-coloured ones look great)
7. 2–3 tbsp tamari or soy sauce
8. 50g baby spinach

Preheat the oven to 100°C fan/120°C/gas ½.

Cut the potatoes in half lengthways, leaving the skins on, and put them into a medium pan. Fill with boiling water, then bring to the boil and cook for 5 minutes. Drain the potatoes in a colander and leave to cool for 5 minutes.

Finely chop the spring onions, and peel and finely chop 1 clove of garlic. Heat 1 tablespoon of olive oil in a medium non-stick pan on a medium heat. Once hot, add the spring onions and garlic and cook for 2–3 minutes, stirring occasionally. Remove from the heat and set aside.

Using a box grater, grate the potatoes into a bowl. Add the cooked spring onions and garlic, along with 1 tablespoon of olive oil, ½ teaspoon of salt and ½ teaspoon of black pepper and mix well. Divide into 8 portions of approx. 80g and flatten into flat discs or patties around 9cm in diameter.

Heat 1 tablespoon of oil in a large non-stick pan over a medium heat. Once hot, add half the hash browns and cook for around 5 minutes on each side, until golden and crispy. Repeat with the rest of the hash browns (keep them warm in the oven).

Add the vegan sausages to the pan for around 4 minutes, until they start to turn golden. Place in the oven to keep warm.

Finely chop the mushrooms and halve the cherry tomatoes, and peel and finely chop the remaining clove of garlic. Put the non-stick pan you used earlier back on a high heat and add the mushrooms. Cook for 4–5 minutes, until they start to turn brown and halve in size. Add the tamari and stir until it is all absorbed.

Add all the cherry tomatoes and the garlic. Cook for a further 4 minutes, then add the baby spinach and cook for a further minute, allowing it to wilt and reduce. Turn off the heat.

Serve the hash browns alongside the vegan sausages and the mushroom mix, with vegan mayo and toast.

Mexican-inspired Potato Rösti Stack

A rösti is a Swiss potato fritter. Here we decided to marry the Swiss and Mexican cuisines to give you a beautiful crispy potato stack with wilted spiced spinach, avocado and a bean salsa. This makes a wonderful weekend breakfast or brunch.

10 INGREDIENTS

1. 1 x 400g tin of black beans

2. 1 large beef tomato

3. 1 avocado

4. 15g fresh coriander

5. 2 limes

6. 400g potatoes

7. 1 tbsp self-raising flour

8. 1 tbsp cumin seeds

9. 200g baby spinach

10. 1 red chilli

To make the bean salsa, drain and rinse the black beans and slice the tomato into 1–2cm cubes. Cut the avocado in half, remove the stone, then scoop out the flesh and cut it into approx. 1–2cm cubes. Finely chop the fresh coriander, setting aside 1 tablespoon for garnish. Put the beans, avocado, tomato and coriander into a large bowl, along with ¾ teaspoon of salt and ¼ teaspoon of black pepper, 1 tablespoon of olive oil and the juice of 1 lime. Mix well and adjust the seasoning to your palate.

Leaving the skins on, grate the potatoes on the wide part of a box grater. Put them into a sieve, add a pinch of salt, then mix and squeeze out any excess water. Put them into a bowl along with the flour, cumin seeds, 1 teaspoon of salt and ¼ teaspoon of black pepper. Mix well.

Shape into four equal-sized small patties approx. 80g each, and flatten them into rounds 10cm in diameter. Heat 1 tablespoon of oil in a non-stick frying pan on a high heat. Once hot, reduce the heat to medium, add the röstis and fry for 5 minutes on each side until golden brown. Transfer to kitchen paper to dry. Continue until all the röstis are cooked.

While the röstis are frying, wilt the spinach. Heat a medium saucepan on a high heat and add 2 tablespoons of water, along with the spinach, a pinch of salt, the juice of ½ a lime and a pinch of black pepper. Put a lid on the pan and leave to wilt for 2–3 minutes. Remove, taste and add more salt and pepper if it needs it.

Put 2 röstis on each plate, add a layer of wilted spinach and top with the bean salsa. Finely slice the chilli and sprinkle over the top, and serve with the remaining ½ lime, cut in quarters. Garnish with the remaining chopped fresh coriander.

Spicy Smashed Potatoes with Sriracha Mayo

We are going to be bold here and say that this is possibly the nicest way to eat a potato! Being Irish, potatoes have a very special place in our hearts. Some say we eat so many potatoes they are flowing in our blood. These are so magnificent, so crispy, so crunchy and so tasty! If you're short of time, just use store-bought vegan mayo and sriracha sauce.

6 INGREDIENTS

1. 1kg baby or floury potatoes

2. 1 tbsp tamari or soy sauce

3. 3 tbsp sriracha sauce (page 274)

4. ½ tbsp maple syrup

5. 1 tsp garlic powder

6. 5 tbsp vegan mayo (page 275)

Preheat the oven to 200°C fan/220°C/gas 7.

Chop the potatoes into similar-sized pieces about the size of a squash ball, leaving the skins on. If using baby potatoes, leave them whole. In a pan of boiling water, boil the potatoes for 15–20 minutes, until a knife pierces them easily but they are not falling apart. Once they are ready, drain them.

Coat a baking tray with 1 tablespoon of olive oil. Transfer the boiled potatoes to the baking tray and gently flatten them with the base of a glass/mug or pot. Be careful here not to smash them too much but ensure they open up and expose their starchy centres!

In a bowl, whisk together 5 tablespoons of olive oil with the tamari, 1 tablespoon of sriracha (if you like), maple syrup and garlic powder.

Using a pastry brush, brush the oil mixture evenly over the smashed potatoes, making sure you coat each one. Sprinkle evenly with ½ teaspoon of salt and ¼ teaspoon of pepper.

Roast for 25–30 minutes in the oven, until golden and super-crispy.

For the sriracha mayo, simply mix the mayo with 2 tablespoons of sriracha. Remove the roasted smashed potatoes from the oven and serve with the sriracha dip. Enjoy!

Creamy Leek and Potato Pies

Scrumptious little savoury pies that are creamy, crispy and oh, so yummy. They work well as party food, as a starter, as a side or for dinner with roasted veg and salad. These pies are great to freeze and make a lovely cold lunch too. You will need a muffin tray to bake them.

9 INGREDIENTS

1. 3 or 4 x 320g sheets of vegan puff pastry

2. 400g potatoes of choice

3. 1 leek, approx. 300g

4. 2 garlic cloves

5. 75g vegan Cheddar cheese

6. 4 tbsp plain white flour

7. 400ml oat milk or non-dairy milk of choice

8. ½ tsp garlic powder

9. 1 tsp mustard

If you are using frozen puff pastry, make sure it has thawed. Preheat the oven to 180°C fan/200°C/gas 6. Lightly oil 15 holes in two muffin trays.

Cut the potatoes into ½cm pieces, leaving the skins on. Halve the leek lengthways, then cut it into 1cm pieces, including the green parts, and give them a good wash. Peel and finely chop the garlic. Grate the vegan Cheddar.

Put a non-stick wide-bottomed pan on a high heat and add 1 tablespoon of olive oil. Once hot, add the leek and potatoes. Cook for 5 minutes, stirring occasionally, then add the garlic and cook for a further 5 minutes, stirring regularly. Turn the heat down to medium, add a good pinch of salt and put a lid on the pan – this will allow the veg to cook in their own juices. Cook for 10 minutes, stirring occasionally.

To make the béchamel sauce, put 4 tablespoons of olive oil into a pan on a medium heat. Once hot, sieve in the flour and cook for 1–2 minutes, stirring continuously with a whisk until it goes slightly golden. Slowly add the oat milk, stirring continuously. Bring to the boil, then reduce to a gentle simmer, stirring to be careful that nothing sticks to the bottom. Add a pinch of salt, a pinch of ground black pepper, the garlic powder and the mustard, and mix well. Once simmering, and when it reaches a creamy texture, remove from the heat. Taste and adjust the seasoning if it needs it.

Add the potatoes and leeks to the creamy béchamel sauce and leave to cool before filling the pastry (otherwise it will tear).

Unroll the pastry on to a lightly floured work surface. Using a 12cm cookie cutter, cut 15 pastry circles and gently push these into the oiled muffin holes. Cut 15 pie tops out of the remaining pastry with a 10cm cutter and set aside in the fridge while you fill the pies.

Fill the pastry casings with the potato and leek mixture, approx. 2–3 tablespoons of filling in each. Top with the pastry circles. Trim any longer corner pieces of pastry, then pinch together the bottom and top pieces of pastry to seal the pie. Using a pastry brush, brush each pie with oat milk to encourage it to turn golden. Bake in the oven for 30 minutes.

Serve as a starter, or with some roasted veg and salad for a main course.

POTATOES

Creamy Dauphinoise Potatoes

When we were growing up, Dad used to make a variation of this for special occasions – it was such a treat! Here we make a simple plant-based version of the French classic. This may look like it takes a long time, but the oven does all the hard work and it makes a wonderful side dish.

8 INGREDIENTS

1. 125g vegan Cheddar cheese

2. 3 sprigs of fresh thyme

3. 1kg white waxy potatoes

4. 3 cloves of garlic

5. 4 tbsp plain white flour

6. 500ml oat milk, or non-dairy milk of choice

7. 1 x 400ml tin of coconut milk

8. 40g fresh breadcrumbs

Preheat the oven to 180°C fan/200°C/gas 6.

Grate the cheese and pick the thyme leaves from their stems. Cut the potatoes lengthways in half, leaving the skins on, and put them into a medium saucepan. Cover with boiling water, bring to the boil, then reduce to a simmer for 12 minutes until they are three-quarters cooked but not falling apart. Drain the potatoes and leave to cool.

While the potatoes are cooking, peel and finely chop the garlic, then make the creamy béchamel sauce.

To do this, put 4 tablespoons of olive oil into a pan on a medium heat. Once hot, add the diced garlic and reduce the heat so it doesn't burn and cook for 1–2 minutes. Sieve in the flour and cook for another 1–2 minutes, stirring continuously with a whisk until it goes slightly golden. Slowly add the oat milk, stirring continuously. Bring to the boil, then reduce to a gentle simmer, stirring to be careful that nothing sticks to the bottom. Add ½ teaspoon of salt, a generous pinch of ground black pepper and 50g of the vegan Cheddar and mix well. Once simmering, add the cream layer from the tin of coconut milk and whisk until incorporated. Continue to simmer until it reaches a creamy texture, then remove from the heat. Taste and adjust the seasoning if it needs it. (The remaining coconut water can be used as a base for a smoothie, or as a stock or soup.)

Cut the potatoes into 1cm-thick slices. Make an even layer of the sliced potatoes in the bottom of a deep oven dish approx. 22 x 22cm. Add a layer of the béchamel to cover just this layer of potato. Add another even layer of potato, followed by another layer of the béchamel. Repeat this process until the dish is full, saving enough sauce for the top layer, so the potatoes are totally covered. You should get three layers of potatoes in a 22 x 22cm dish.

Mix the rest of the grated vegan Cheddar with the breadcrumbs and scatter over the casserole dish along with the thyme leaves. Bake in the oven for 20–25 minutes, until the sauce has thickened and is bubbling. The top will be browned and the potatoes will be cooked through. Serve as a side with any of your favourite mains.

Creamy Potato and Kale Croquettes with Umami Mayo

Crispy on the outside, and soft and gooey on the inside, these are a great way to get more veg into kids! Croquette in French means crunch and that is what we want here. This makes wonderful party food, and will be one of the first to go on a buffet. They also work well as a lovely side dish, and are great served with baked beans and some greens as a main meal.

9 INGREDIENTS

1. 500g potatoes of choice

2. 100g kale

3. 75g vegan Cheddar cheese

4. 200ml vegan mayo (page 275), or store-bought vegan mayo

5. 1 tbsp tamari or soy sauce

6. 50g sesame seeds

7. 50g fresh breadcrumbs

8. 50ml oat milk or non-dairy milk of choice

9. 50g plain white flour

Cut the potatoes into bite-size pieces, leaving the skins on, and put them into a medium saucepan on a high heat. Cover with boiling water and add a generous pinch of salt. Bring to the boil, then reduce to a simmer for 10–12 minutes, until the potatoes are tender. Drain the potatoes, ensuring you remove any excess moisture, and put them back into the pot.

Remove the stems from the kale and finely chop the leaves. Add them to the pan of boiled potatoes and mash them together. Put back on a low heat for 2 minutes to evaporate any extra water, then remove from the heat and set aside.

Grate the vegan Cheddar and add it to the mashed potatoes along with ½ teaspoon of salt and ¼ teaspoon of black pepper. Taste and add more seasoning if it needs it.

Divide the mashed potato mixture into 14 small balls, approx. 45g each, and put them into the freezer for 5 minutes while you prepare the other ingredients.

For the umami mayo, mix the vegan mayo and tamari together and set aside.

In a bowl, mix the sesame seeds and breadcrumbs together with a pinch of salt. Put the oat milk and flour into two separate bowls.

Remove the potato balls from the freezer and shape them into small sausage shapes approx. 5cm long.

Dip each one into the flour first and coat evenly, then into the oat milk, and lastly coat in the breadcrumb and sesame seed mixture.

Heat 3 tablespoons of oil in a large non-stick frying pan on a medium heat. Carefully add the croquettes and fry until they are golden all over. Remove from the heat and serve with the umami mayo.

POTATOES

Chickpea, Potato and Pesto Bake

This recipe is in honour of our friend the great José Lopez, who worked in the café for a few years. He was the most colourful, vibrant human you could ever meet, and he always called this 'cheese pea base' instead of chickpea bake! It's a beautiful, simple chickpea stew with sliced potato and a rich pesto topping.

9 INGREDIENTS

1. 2 red onions

2. 2 large cloves of garlic

3. 2 carrots

4. 1 x 400g tin of chickpeas

5. 700g potatoes of choice

6. 2 x 400g tins of chopped tomatoes

7. 1½ tsp smoked paprika

8. 2 tbsp maple syrup

9. 200g red pepper and almond pesto (page 273), or pesto of choice

Preheat the oven to 180°C fan/200°C/gas 6.

Peel and finely chop the red onions and garlic. Slice the carrots into thin rounds. Drain and rinse the chickpeas.

Cut the potatoes in half lengthways, leaving the skins on. Put them into a medium pan and cover with boiling water. Add 1 tablespoon of salt, bring to the boil, then reduce to a simmer for 15 minutes. Once the potatoes are tender but not mushy, drain them and carefully cut them lengthways into slices approx. 1cm wide.

While the potatoes are cooking, heat 1 tablespoon of olive oil in a large saucepan or frying pan on a high heat. Once hot, add the onions, carrots and a pinch of salt. Fry for 4–5 minutes, stirring regularly, until the onions start to brown around the edges. Add the garlic and fry for 1 minute, stirring regularly.

Add the tinned tomatoes, chickpeas, smoked paprika, maple syrup, 3 tablespoons of pesto, 1½ teaspoons of salt and a generous pinch of black pepper. Bring to the boil, then reduce the heat and simmer with the lid on for 10 minutes, stirring occasionally. Remove from the heat.

Pour the tomato and chickpea sauce into a casserole dish approx. 20 x 30 x 5cm. Make an even layer of sliced potatoes over the chickpea mixture and spread the remaining pesto on top.

Bake in the oven for 15 minutes, until the pesto and potatoes start to turn golden and smell amazing!

Serve with some green salad leaves.

Spiced Jackfruit and Potato 'Chops'

These are often served at weddings and parties in Goa, in southern India, and are called 'chops'. Here we use spiced jackfruit to contrast with the soft creamy potato and the crispy exterior. They go great as a starter or as party food served with sriracha sauce (page 274).

10 INGREDIENTS

1. 1 x 400g tin of jackfruit

2. 1 red onion

3. 1 clove of garlic

4. 10g fresh ginger

5. 15g fresh coriander or basil

6. 1kg potatoes of choice

7. 4 tbsp barbecue sauce (page 276)

8. 6 tbsp sriracha sauce (page 274)

9. 50ml oat milk

10. 100g fresh breadcrumbs

Drain and rinse the jackfruit, then roughly chop, removing any hard seeds. Peel and dice the onion, garlic and ginger. Finely chop the fresh coriander or basil.

Cut the potatoes into bite-size pieces, leaving the skins on, then put them into a saucepan with 1 tablespoon of salt and cover with boiling water. Bring to the boil, then reduce to a simmer for 15 minutes.

Meanwhile, heat 1 tablespoon of olive oil in a large non-stick frying pan on a high heat. Once hot, add the onion, jackfruit and a pinch of salt. Fry for 6–7 minutes, stirring occasionally, until the onion starts to brown. Add the garlic and ginger and cook for a further minute.

Reduce the heat to medium. Add the barbecue sauce, 2 tablespoons of sriracha sauce and the chopped coriander or basil, and mix well. Cook for a minute more, then remove from the heat and stir well. Adjust the seasoning to your liking and leave to cool.

When the potatoes are tender but not overcooked, drain them and leave with the lid off, so that any extra moisture evaporates. Mash the potatoes with a potato masher, along with 1 teaspoon of salt, ½ teaspoon of black pepper and 3 tablespoons of oil. Taste and add more salt and pepper if it needs it. Leave the potatoes to cool for 5 minutes.

Take 4 tablespoons of potato, approx. 65g, and shape into a ball. Using your thumb, gently create a hollow in the centre of the ball and stuff it with 1 tablespoon of the jackfruit filling. Cover with mashed potato and place on a baking tray. Carefully flatten to a burger shape, approx. 4–5cm in diameter. Repeat to make 14 chops and then chill them in the fridge for 5 minutes. Keep any remaining filling to serve.

Put the oat milk and breadcrumbs into two separate bowls. Dip each chop first into the oat milk and then into the breadcrumbs.

Heat 2 tablespoons of oil in a non-stick frying pan on a medium heat. Add 5 chops at a time and fry until golden brown on both sides. This should take around 3–4 minutes per side. Remove and place on kitchen paper to drain. Repeat until all the chops are crispy and golden.

Serve hot or warm, with the remaining 4 tablespoons of sriracha sauce or any leftover jackfruit as a nice accompaniment!

POTATOES

Comforting Easy Cottage Pie

This is a hearty, wholesome, nourishing dish that is also packed with flavour and fibre. It is pretty straightforward – if you want to make it more indulgent you could spread some pesto on top of the potato once you take it out of the oven.

10 INGREDIENTS

1. 6 medium potatoes
2. 2 red onions
3. 2 cloves of garlic
4. 2 carrots
5. 1 medium leek
6. 2 x 400g tins of lentils
7. 1 x 400g tin of chopped tomatoes
8. 4 tbsp tamari or soy sauce
9. 125ml oat milk, or non-dairy milk of choice
10. 75g vegan Cheddar cheese

Preheat the oven to 200°C fan/220°C/gas 7.

Roughly chop the potatoes into similar-sized pieces, leaving their skins on. Put them into a pan with a good pinch of salt and cover with water. Bring to the boil, then turn down to a simmer for 10–15 minutes, until they are tender.

While the potatoes are boiling, peel and finely chop the onions and garlic, and chop the carrots into thin rounds. Chop the leek into approx. 2cm chunks, including the green parts, and give them a good wash. Drain and rinse the lentils.

Put a wide-bottomed non-stick pan on a high heat. Once hot, add 1 tablespoon of oil and leave it to heat up for a minute. Add the onions, leek and carrots along with 1 teaspoon of salt. Cook for 3–4 minutes, stirring regularly. Add the garlic and cook for a further 3–4 minutes, stirring regularly. Add the lentils, the tinned tomatoes, ½ teaspoon of black pepper and the tamari. Bring to the boil, then reduce to a simmer for 5 minutes or until the carrots are cooked through. Remove from the heat and adjust the seasoning to your liking.

Once the potatoes are cooked, drain them and put them back into the pan. Mash, using a potato masher, until they reach a smooth consistency. Add 1½ teaspoons of salt, ½ teaspoon of black pepper and most of the oat milk while mashing – just enough so that it mashes easily but doesn't get sloppy. Taste and add more salt and pepper if you think it needs it.

Transfer the lentil mixture into a casserole dish (20 x 30 x 5cm) and top with the mashed potato. As the lentil mixture is quite wet, it's best to spoon out the mashed potato across the full area of the lentil mix one spoon at a time and spread it out that way, rather than piling it all into the middle and trying to spread it to the edges.

Grate the vegan cheese and sprinkle it over the top, then bake in the oven for 20 minutes or until the top starts to crisp.

Serve with some green salad leaves.

Spinach, Potato and Coconut Curry

Inspired by saag aloo, or spinach and potato curry, this is a really hearty dish in which the spinach melts to give an almost creamy texture. It might seem like a huge amount of spinach but it cooks down a lot, so just have patience. We like this with rice or pitta breads.

10 INGREDIENTS

1. 1 onion
2. 2 cloves of garlic
3. ½ a thumb-size piece of fresh ginger
4. 500g potatoes of choice
5. 1 red chilli
6. 1 tsp black mustard seeds
7. 1 tsp cumin seeds
8. 1 x 400ml tin of coconut milk
9. 600g fresh or frozen spinach
10. 1 lime

Peel and finely chop the onion, garlic and ginger. Chop the potatoes into small bite-size pieces, leaving the skins on. Finely slice the red chilli.

Put a large non-stick frying pan on a high heat. Once hot, add 1 tablespoon of olive oil, the chopped onion and a pinch of salt. Fry for 4 minutes, stirring occasionally. Add the chopped ginger and garlic, reduce the heat to medium and fry for a further 2 minutes. Add the cumin and black mustard seeds and cook for 1–2 minutes, until the cumin seeds start to pop.

Add the chopped potatoes and a pinch of salt. Mix well, then put a lid on the pan and cook for 8 minutes, stirring occasionally to prevent the veg burning.

Add the coconut milk, spinach, 1 teaspoon of salt and ½ teaspoon of black pepper. Cook on a medium heat until the spinach starts to wilt. Bring to the boil and leave to simmer with the lid on for 10–15 minutes, stirring regularly. You want the spinach to have broken down and be adding a creamy feel to the sauce.

Add the juice of the lime and mix through.

Garnish with the red chilli and serve with rice or toasted wholemeal pitta breads.

POTATOES

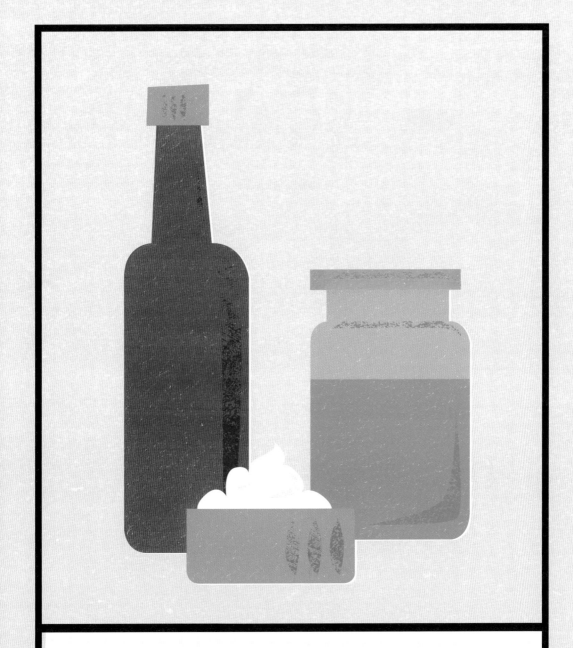

SAUCES AND DIPS

Wine and Thyme Gravy

This is an easy-to-make gravy based on veg stock, with a wine reduction, umami notes and some thyme to add a lovely subtle depth of flavour. It is simple to make ahead of time and heat up before serving. We serve it with the rich and creamy mushroom Wellington on page 243.

7 INGREDIENTS

1. 4 shallots or 1 medium onion

2. 2 cloves of garlic

3. 3 sprigs of fresh thyme

4. 400ml veg stock

5. 2 tbsp tamari or soy sauce

6. 100ml red wine

7. 3 tbsp cornflour or plain white flour

Peel and finely chop the shallots/onion and garlic. Remove the fresh thyme leaves from the stalks.

Heat 1½ tablespoons of oil in a small non-stick pan on a high heat. Once hot, add the shallots and cook for 4–5 minutes, stirring regularly, until they start to turn golden. Add the chopped garlic and fry for 1 minute more.

In a large jug, mix together the veg stock, tamari, red wine, thyme leaves and a pinch of black pepper. Pour into the pan and bring to the boil, then reduce the heat down to a gentle simmer.

Put 4 tablespoons of this stock mixture into a mug and sieve in the cornflour. Mix well, then add to the pan. Add 2 tablespoons of oil and cook for a further 3–4 minutes.

Pour the gravy through a sieve placed over a 1-litre jug. For a thicker consistency and stronger taste, you can leave the mixture to simmer for longer to concentrate it. If it tastes too strong, just dilute it by adding a little boiling water to reach your desired taste and texture.

Mushroom Gravy

This is a really wonderful and easy gravy that goes great with pies and pastry dishes. We also find it goes well on sandwiches, and in fact with most savoury food!

7 INGREDIENTS

1. 150g oyster mushrooms, or mushrooms of choice

2. 1 medium onion

3. 2 tbsp tamari or soy sauce

4. 500ml veg stock

5. 1 tsp garlic powder

6. 3 tbsp nutritional yeast

7. 2 tbsp cornflour

Cut the mushrooms into strips and roughly chop the onion.

Heat 2 tablespoons of oil in a medium, non-stick, wide-bottomed pan on a high heat. Spread the mushrooms in a single layer in the pan, then flatten with the base of another clean pan for a few minutes and remove. Leave the mushrooms cooking over a medium heat for 6–10 minutes, or until all the liquid has cooked off and the mushrooms get a nice caramelized brown colour. You will be tempted to stir, but try not to! Though at the same time do check them so that they don't burn. Add the tamari and a pinch of black pepper and mix well, making sure you incorporate any bits that have stuck to the bottom of the pan. Remove the mushrooms from the pan and set aside.

Deglaze the pan by adding 6 tablespoons of the veg stock over a high heat, stirring with a wooden spoon until all the remaining mushroom bits are mixed with the stock. Set this aside to be added to the gravy.

Heat 1 tablespoon of oil in a medium non-stick pan on a high heat. Once hot, add the onions, then reduce the heat to medium and cook for 3–5 minutes, stirring regularly until they start to turn golden.

Mix the mushroom stock (from the deglazing), the rest of the veg stock, the garlic powder, nutritional yeast and a pinch of black pepper in a large jug (the mushrooms don't get added at this point), then pour into the pan. Bring to the boil, then reduce the heat to a gentle simmer. Strain through a mesh sieve to remove the onions, and return the stock to the pan.

Remove 5 tablespoons of the sauce to the jug and sift in the cornflour, whisking well so it is fully incorporated and there are no lumps. Put it back into the pan.

Add 4 tablespoons of oil to the pan and simmer for 3–4 minutes until it thickens, whisking occasionally. Now add your meaty mushrooms to the gravy, et voilà, you have a wonderful mushroom gravy!

Harissa Sauce

Harissa is a rockin' hot paste with its roots in Tunisia and is widely used in other countries in North Africa. You are likely to find as many versions of it as you are people who make it, so there really is no one perfect recipe. Some add caraway seeds and others red peppers, tomato purée or lemon. Ours is a sweet, spicy, salty and delicious dip that goes well with everything. We use it in the baked spiced harissa aubergine with a chunky salsa on page 67.

5 INGREDIENTS

1. 5 fresh red chillies

2. 6 sun-dried tomatoes

3. 2 cloves of garlic

4. 1 tsp chilli flakes

5. 1½ tsp salt

Preheat the oven to 220°C fan/240°C/gas 9.

Chop the tops off the chillies and cut them in half lengthways, leaving the seeds in. Bake them in the oven for 10 minutes.

Meanwhile soak the sun-dried tomatoes in boiling water for 5 minutes, then drain.

Once the chillies are done, put them into a food processor with the drained sun-dried tomatoes, 4 tablespoons of olive oil and the rest of the ingredients, and blend until smooth.

Store in an airtight jar or a tub and it will keep for at least 2 weeks in your fridge.

MAKES approx. 450g   TAKES 5 minutes

Red Pepper and Almond Pesto

This is a wonderfully vibrant pesto that we adore slightly chunky so you can see its components. It goes great with pasta, on sandwiches, on baked potatoes – on most things really!

7 INGREDIENTS

1. 10g garlic (approx. 1 large clove)

2. 30g fresh basil leaves

3. 100g roasted red peppers, from a jar

4. 100g whole almonds

5. 150ml olive oil

6. 15ml balsamic vinegar

7. 10ml lemon juice

Peel the garlic and remove any tough stalks from the basil. Drain and rinse the red peppers.

Put all the ingredients into a food processor with 1 teaspoon of salt and blend. If you want your pesto chunky, pulse it until it reaches your desired consistency. If you want it super-smooth, blend for longer until it becomes creamy.

Taste and add more salt or lemon juice if it needs it.

The pesto will keep for 2 weeks in a sealed container in the fridge.

Sriracha Sauce

Normally sriracha is fermented for a few days to build up some natural acidity; however, we did some blind-taste tests and found that we preferred this 10-minute version on flavour and also that it saved us time! Sriracha is a sweet, spicy, slightly acidic condiment that adds flavour to any dish.

6 INGREDIENTS

1. 240g fresh red chillies

2. 50g sugar (we use caster)

3. 3 cloves of garlic

4. 65ml apple cider vinegar

5. 1 tbsp sparkling water

6. 1½ tbsp arrowroot powder

Remove the stalks from the chillies but keep the green tops.

Put the chillies into a blender with the sugar, garlic and ½ teaspoon of salt, and blend until smooth. Add the vinegar, sparkling water and arrowroot powder and blend again until smooth.

Strain through a mesh strainer over a medium pan, pushing the pulp through to extract all the liquid.

Put the pan on a medium heat and bring to a simmer for 8 minutes, stirring regularly to prevent burning. Simmer until the sauce thickens. Remove from the heat and store in an airtight container. It will keep for 2–3 weeks in the fridge.

MAKES 600g   TAKES 15 minutes

Vegan Mayonnaise

You may have come across this recipe of ours before, but it is so good that we use it in a few of the recipes in this book and so we had to include it. It is a super-tasty mayo, which is just like the real thing, easy to make and goes splendidly with just about everything!

6 INGREDIENTS

1. 300ml soy milk

2. 2 tbsp lemon juice

3. 1 tsp garlic powder

4. ¼ tsp ground black pepper

5. 1 tbsp Dijon mustard

6. 300ml vegetable oil (ideally neutral-tasting)

Put all the ingredients except the oil into a blender, add ½ teaspoon of salt and blend for 1 minute.

While the blender is on, slowly add the oil until the mix emulsifies. Blend until you reach a wonderful mayonnaise consistency.

Stored in an airtight container in the fridge, this will keep for 3 weeks.

Barbecue Sauce

This is such an easy and versatile sauce – it adds instant flavour to any dish you are making!

9 INGREDIENTS

Simply mix all of the ingredients together. The sauce will keep for 2 weeks in the fridge.

1. 2 tsp smoked paprika

2. 1 tsp of dried garlic powder/½ fresh clove of garlic, finely chopped

3. 4 tbsp tamari/ soy sauce

4. 2 tbsp tomato purée

5. 2 tbsp cider vinegar

6. 2 tbsp oil

7. 4 tbsp water

8. 2 tsp maple syrup/agave syrup

9. ¼ tsp chilli powder/ cayenne pepper

Recipe notes

Index

Acknowledgements

Although our names are down as the authors of this book, it has really been a product of so many people's hard work. We are standing on the shoulders of a lot of wonderful people who all helped bring this book together.

First and foremost, thanks to our families for their support – you are our heart in so many ways. Thanks to Justyna, May, Theo and Ned; Sabrina, Elsie, Issy and Janet.

Special thanks to our Mom and Dad, Donal and Ismay, for without you both none of this would be possible. Thanks for the constant encouragement and inspiration and for always being there when we need support; Mom, thanks for caring so much and for often doing the less glamorous but vital jobs!

Dad, thanks for always being there to advise and to guide us and The Happy Pear, we are eternally grateful.

Massive thanks to our brothers Mark and Darragh. Darragh, you are the unsung hero of The Happy Pear but so rarely get the recognition and limelight you deserve. We're very lucky to be your brothers. Mark, it's fabulous to have you back in the team colours! We're loving seeing you so much and working beside you again, thanks for being you, for being so straight, so cool and level-headed.

Thanks to Naomi Dooge for being an amazing home economist on this book and beyond: developing, testing, trialling and iterating recipes and ideas, thanks for being so wonderful to work with so closely, for being so professional as well as such a good, wise friend over all these years! Seanie Cahill, thanks for the friendship, it's always wonderful to work with you, thanks for the inspiration, constant support and for always being there. Thanks for being so patient with us and for doing such a good job with all our videos, podcasts and content creation!

Thanks to Paul Murphy for all your support and hard work in running the HP with Darragh and us. Thanks for always having our backs and for having such a complementary skillset to us! We are very grateful to work with you and have you on the HP team.

Thanks to Sara Fawsitt, 'the third twin', for being amazing, for helping organize our lives, for having our back, for juggling so many balls and for caring so much. You are a dear friend, 'twin sister', and we are so grateful that you work with us – you are a true powerhouse and we love working with you! Thanks for everything.

Thanks to all the wonderful team at Penguin Life – as always you have been so lovely to work with. First, thanks to Amy, our lovely editor on this book along with Emily (we hope maternity leave goes well). Thanks to Julia, Corinna and Kayla for being a part of this book from the start. Thanks to Joanna Prior and Tom again for trusting in us. Thanks to the art department for putting so much effort into this book – Richard, you've been a joy to work with, we love how collaborative you are and open to getting our input and for being good craic too! Thanks to Saffron for leading the design and wonderful styling of this book, you are fab at what you do and hope the new house goes well! A big thanks to our copy-editor Annie, and to all the wider Penguin team who have worked hard to make this book a success: Natalie, Hannah, Annie, Olivia, Louise, Rachel, Sam and Carrie.

Thanks to Maja Smend and her assistants for the beautiful photos, to Maud Eden who did such a great job styling the photos in some interesting times, and to Rob Merrett for the brilliant prop styling.

Thanks to our agent, Faith O'Grady – we really value your help and guidance.

Next, thanks to the fantastic team that makes The Happy Pear what it is. Without you there would be no Happy Pear. Our HP team in Church Road, in Pearville, on the farm and online. Thank you for caring, we are most grateful.

Thanks to all the Happy Pear team that have come and gone over the years; you have all had an impact on what it is.

Thanks to our wonderful training and swim rise crew; you enrich our lives in so many ways.

Finally, thanks to the people of our hometown of Greystones and our extended community – thank you for your support, without it there would be no Happy Pear!

Dave & Steve xx

PENGUIN LIFE

UK | USA | Canada | Ireland | Australia
India | New Zealand | South Africa

Penguin Life is part of the Penguin Random House group of companies
whose addresses can be found at global.penguinrandomhouse.com.

First published 2022
001

Photography © Maja Smend, except p. 45 © Stephen Flynn
Colour reproduction by Altaimage Ltd
Printed in Italy by Printer Trento s.r.l.

The authorized representative in the EEA is Penguin Random House Ireland,
Morrison Chambers, 32 Nassau Street, Dublin DO2 YH68

A CIP catalogue record for this book is available from the British Library

ISBN: 978–0–241–53524–0

www.greenpenguin.co.uk

Penguin Random House is committed to a
sustainable future for our business, our readers
and our planet. This book is made from Forest
Stewardship Council® certified paper.